The Seven Habits of
the Good Life

The Seven Habits of the Good Life

How the Biblical Virtues Free Us from the Seven Deadly Sins

Kalman J. Kaplan
and Matthew B. Schwartz

ROWMAN & LITTLEFIELD PUBLISHERS, INC.
Lanham • Boulder • New York • Toronto • Oxford

ROWMAN & LITTLEFIELD PUBLISHERS, INC.

Published in the United States of America
by Rowman & Littlefield Publishers, Inc.
A wholly owned subsidiary of The Rowman & Littlefield Publishing Group, Inc.
4501 Forbes Boulevard, Suite 200, Lanham, Maryland 20706
www.rowmanlittlefield.com

PO Box 317, Oxford
OX2 9RU, UK

Distributed by National Book Network

British Library Cataloguing in Publication Information Available

Library of Congress Cataloging-in-Publication Data

Kaplan, Kalman J.
    The seven habits of the good life : how the biblical virtues free us from the seven
    deadly sins / Kalman J. Kaplan and Matthew B. Schwartz.
        p.   cm.
    Includes bibliographical references and index.
    ISBN-13: 978-0-7425-3274-8 (cloth : alk. paper)
    ISBN-10: 0-7425-3274-7 (cloth : alk. paper)
    1. Virtues—Biblical teaching.   2. Bible—Psychology.   3. Deadly sins.
I. Schwartz, Matthew B.   II. Title.
BS680.V56K37   2006
296.7—dc22   2006007499

Printed in the United States of America

∞ ™ The paper used in this publication meets the minimum requirements of American
National Standard for Information Sciences—Permanence of Paper for Printed Library
Materials, ANSI/NISO Z39.48-1992.

To my grandson, Levi Judah Kaplan,
the best Biblical gift that one could ask for,
and to his parents who brought him into the world.
Kalman J. Kaplan

To the young lady from Scheveningen.
Matthew B. Schwartz

Contents

Acknowledgments

We would like to express our profound appreciation to Jim Langford for the encouragement and help he has given us throughout the preparation of this book. He has inspired us, guided us and even edited our excesses. We could not have completed this book without Jim's help and we are deeply grateful to him. We are grateful to John Loudon, executive editor of Rowman and Littlefield, who has steered this project to completion. Our thanks also to many other members of the editorial staff at Rowman and Littlefield, including especially Ross Miller and Sarah Johnson. Katherine Macdonald and Nancy Doherty are likewise marvelous editors.

Introduction

"To know wisdom and instruction, to perceive the words of understanding; to receive the instruction of wisdom, justice, judgment and equity; to give prudence to the simple, to the young man knowledge and discretion."

—Proverbs 1:1–4

This book is written to unbind the Bible as a guide to the way we live our everyday lives. An ancient Hebrew saying emphasizes the importance of three factors in assessing a person's character: *caaso, coso* and *ciso,* referring respectively to how a person handles his anger (*caaso*), his drinking (*coso*) and his spending (*ciso*). We will discuss Biblical gifts with regard to seven problem areas, including the above three, showing how each of these is essential in freeing us to live our lives in fuller and less conflicted ways. Seven is a number often used in the Bible. God created the world in six days, and on the seventh day, He rested. People may work their fields for six years, but the seventh is a sabbatical year when the land rests fallow. The candelabra in the Temple had seven branches. Noah brought seven species of each pure animal onto the ark. The Talmud lists seven legal norms (i.e., Noachide laws) binding upon all humanity: 1) a requirement of the establishment of a system of civil law, plus prohibitions against 2) blasphemy, 3) idolatry, 4) murder, 5) robbery, 6) sexual immorality, and 7) the eating of flesh torn from a living animal (*Babylonian Talmud*, Sanhedrin 56a). The Book of Proverbs provides yet another example of the number seven:

> Six things the Lord hates,
> Seven things are detestable to him:

> A proud eye, a false tongue,
> Hands that shed innocent blood
> A heart that forges thoughts of mischief,
> And feet that run swiftly to do evil,
> A false witness telling a pack of lies,
> And one who stirs up quarrels between brothers.
> Proverbs 6:16–19

The number seven has become etched in our imagination. Indeed, John Cassian of Marseilles and Pope Gregory the Great introduced the idea of Seven Deadly Sins: pride, envy, anger, lust, gluttony, greed and sloth. Each of these sins clearly is the sign of an unbalanced personality, in ways which we shall describe shortly. However, the antidotes offered to these sins are often unbalanced, representing simply the opposite side of the same coin.

In his fifth-century poem, *Psychomachia*, for example, Prudentius describes a battlefield in which each of these sins is confronted in combat by a corresponding virtue. Dante Alighieri, writing in the thirteenth century, treats these sins in his descriptions of Hell and Purgatory. It is entirely possible that the focus on sin actually derived from the widespread beliefs in superstition—magic, astrology and demons. People became terrified of powers that they could not control, including personality characteristics they regarded as dangerous. The only way to oppose them was by gaining power over them. Thus the sin of pride was met by the virtue humility, envy was met by kindness or liberality, anger by patience (Prudentius) or peace (Dante), lust by chastity, gluttony by abstinence, greed by wastefulness, and sloth by zeal.

It may well be that Prudentius intended these virtues to moderate the extremes inherent in the seven sins. However, these antidotes can be seen as polar opposites of the vices, equally imbalanced in the opposite direction, and no healthier than the sins that they are combating.

Part of the problem lies in the oppositional view of self and other that is so prevalent in modern society. According to this view, intimacy with another is only achieved at the price of loss of self and of space for oneself. Moderation or balance is seen as the only solution, no matter how unsatisfactory. This very restricted view opens the door to all sorts of possible confusions and misinterpretations. Does one seek the company of ("nearness" to) others because of a genuine concern for them (let us call this attachment), or because of a desire to run away from oneself (let us call this de-individuation)? Consider the following clinical example.

Rich, age twenty-eight, came to marriage therapy focusing on a lack of direction in his life. His complaint that he did not know "where he was going or who he really was" did not seem in character with his behavior with his wife. On the surface Rich seemed affectionate and eager to spend time with his wife. As therapy progressed, however, it became clear that Rich manifested an "infantile clinginess." Seemingly trivial separations became the occasion for panic responses by Rich. The initial impression that Rich was affectionate; i.e., attached, was replaced by a sense that Rich did not know who he was—a lack of individuation.

Likewise "farness" is open to several interpretations. Does one seek solitude to come to know oneself (individuation) or because of a fear of being involved with the other (detachment)? Consider a second clinical example:

Barbara, age twenty-three, entered individual treatment complaining that she did not have close friends. This seemed initially to be a strange complaint because she always seemed to be surrounded by people—both male and female—and immersed in activities. However, in the course of therapy it became clear that she organized her schedule so as to minimize the possibilities for intimate contacts. In fact, she often went to desperate lengths to avoid one-on-one encounters. A superficial analysis suggested that Barbara was individuated. Closer examination, however, indicated a fundamental fear of attachment.

The idea that caring for both self and other are contradictory has led to very ineffective attempts at correction of maladies. One such solution involves the prescription to the person to do the opposite of what he/she is doing. Thus, selfishness is only resolved though merger with others, no matter how unhealthy. Conversely, dependence is only resolved through isolation. In both cases, the antidotes are as polarized as the initial sin. Alternatively, a compromise solution may involve trying to achieve an arithmetic balance between self and other, none of which go to the root of the problem.

Consider Ben, a young attorney who has been dating Laura. It is October and Laura's birthday, but Ben is very busy with a trial. Ben sends his secretary out to get some flowers for Laura, the whole process taking no longer than thirty minutes. When Ben presents the flowers to Laura, she thanks him, but her disappointment is tangible. She expected something more personal. Ben feels guilty that he let Laura down, and resolves to behave differently the next time a gift occasion arises.

Soon it is February and Valentine's Day. This time Ben resolves to do it right. Though he is very busy preparing for another trial, he sets aside an entire week to look for a present for Laura. He knows she likes carpets and he looks in one store after another to search for a carpet that Laura will like. When he finally chooses one, he presents it to Laura, and she is quite happy. However, Ben does not feel so happy. He feels resentful—that he has wasted forty hours of work looking for something in which he is really not personally involved. And Ben takes it out on Laura—in all ways. He comes late for their appointments, criticizes her hairstyle, and generally behaves spitefully.

When Laura's next birthday arrives, Ben is in a quandary. He concludes that looking thirty minutes for a present was too little involvement (leaving him feeling guilty) and forty hours was too much (leaving him feeling like a martyr). So he decides to split the difference. He will look for twenty hours for a present for Laura–not too many (forty hours) and not too little (thirty minutes), but a halfway solution. He looks for a quilt that he thinks Laura will like, but decides to put a limit on how much time he will allot for this. He gets something, which is kind of nice, and Laura kind of likes it. Laura is lukewarm about the gift and Ben in turn feels lukewarm about his efforts. He does not feel too guilty and on the other hand does not feel too martyred. Neither Laura nor Ben feels taken advantage of. However, neither of them feels especially great either.

This is obviously not an ideal solution to the dilemma of self and other. Yet this halfway solution is exactly what many contemporary therapists have recommended. The family therapist Salvatore Minuchin (1974) describes the points of interchange between one member of a family and another. One type of family is enmeshed or over-involved: it has diffuse boundaries. Such a family has difficulty providing sufficient privacy. A disengaged or under-involved family, in contrast, is described as having rigid boundaries. This type of family should have difficulty promoting sufficient communication or intimacy. Minuchin sees healthy families as having clear boundaries, lying in the middle between diffuse boundaries and rigid boundaries. This family should allow for both some privacy and also some communication and intimacy. One should love, but one should not love too much. Not loving enough means the loss of another, but loving too much means a loss of one's self. Ben's solution of looking for twenty hours represents this sort of compromise.

However, this compromise is not really satisfactory. What is wrong with this picture? Simply, love of self is not contradictory to love of other. Ben is not really doing what he wants with his time and Laura is not really getting what she wants. The question becomes: What does Ben want to do with his time? What does Laura want as a gift?

Ben feels fulfilled when he spends time doing what he likes to do and feels he is going through the motions when he is doing things he does not want to do. What does this mean? Ben enjoys time when he enjoys what he is doing. But what sort of time is this? It is self-expressive time. It is time in which Ben expresses something about himself, whether it involves performing in athletics, writing, singing, building a table, cooking, making love or composing a poem. For Ben, it may involve something to do with his song-writing ability. If he can use his time developing and expressing this gift, he will not feel it as a waste, but as expressive well-spent time. If he can give a gift to Laura that is expressive of him, he will not feel the opposition between self and other. The time Ben spends writing Laura a song will be experienced by him as self-expressive. The more time he spends expressing himself to Laura, the better he will feel about himself. He does not have the need to limit the time he spends because it is "alive time"; i.e., time when he feels most alive. Why? Because Ben's giving to Laura involves expressing and strengthening his own personality. Ben is never more himself than when he expresses his love for Laura.

Now, what of Laura? She will value a gift that expresses care on the part of Ben. If Ben gives Laura a song that he has written specifically and expressly for her, she is likely to be very touched. Laura will likely feel that Ben cares enough to really give of himself to her. The opposition of self and other and the implicit struggle over time is broken! Ben's sense of self is not depleted by his love for Laura. Indeed, it is strengthened by his expression of love toward her. And receiving his gift strengthens her sense of self. This resolution does not represent an equivocating moderation which is simply designed to avoid extremes but allows an alternative which emotionally redefines the situation. A harmony can be achieved that is wholehearted and full. It is balanced and not polarized, but it is not moderate in the sense of being only partially committed. One does not have to hold back to be balanced. The more developed the individual, the more fully he/she is capable of loving.

Think of our relationship with God. The Bible begins with a supreme act of love—God's creation of the world. In the Biblical account, God created the world and human beings in an act of love and kindness and has continued to deal with the world in this way ever since. One has only to look at the beauty of creation to feel God's kindness all around. He maintains the movements of heavenly bodies and supplies the wants of even the least of His creatures. Think of the glory of a sunrise, the majesty of a tall mountain, the magnificence of an ocean, along with the wings of a housefly. All the creatures of the world join in a paean of praise to God's loving care. When a person truly recognizes the greatness of God's creation and the depth of his love and kindness, he cannot help but be moved to love the Creator who gave him all these wonders as an act of pure love. Indeed, the Bible expresses this human need in the form of a commandment: "And you shall love the lord your God with all your heart and with all your soul and with all your might." A great person can love greatly!

This book offers seven Biblical habits which can free us from both the deadly sins and their supposed antidotes. These gifts do not idealize moderation per se, but strive for fullness, harmony, and balance. With a loving Creator, one does not need to rebel. Rebellion against Zeus may be called for, but rebellion against the God of the Bible is equivalent to sin and idolatry. This point is vividly made by the prophet Samuel to King Saul in I Samuel 15. Saul had failed to implement fully God's command to destroy the wicked Amalekites. Samuel came to Saul and found King Agag still alive and Saul's soldiers taking spoils. Samuel chastised Saul for rejecting the word of the Lord.

> Hath the Lord as great delight in burnt-offerings and sacrifices,
> As in hearkening to the voice of the Lord?
> Behold, to obey is better than sacrifice,
> And to hearken than the fat of rams.

> For rebellion is as the sin of witchcraft,
> And stubbornness is as idolatry and teraphim.

The seven Biblical virtues, discussed respectively in each of the next seven chapters, are critical in freeing us to live our lives in fuller and less conflicted ways. These gifts represent neither the seven deadly sins nor their antidotes, but instead offer an alternative vision for human personality and behavior. Each of these gifts is based on a non-oppositional view of self and other. The seven Biblical gifts are self-esteem, wisdom, righteousness, love, healthy appetite, prudence, and purpose. Let us juxtapose each of these to the conflict between a deadly sin and its supposed antidote.

The first deadly sin is pride. Pride is defined as a competitive selfishness aimed not only at functioning at full capacity but also at surpassing everyone else. In other words, the problem with pride is that it elevates the self at the expense of the other. The antidote offered for pride has historically been humility. In the proper sense, humility may be a very positive emotional stance of modesty. However, humility has often been equated with worthlessness and a sense of inferiority that elevates the other at the expense of the self. Humility in this sense can be as damaging as pride. The Biblical virtue described in chapter 1 is neither pride nor humility, but a genuine self-esteem that depends not on being better than someone else or, conversely, worse than someone else. It is based on the sense that each person is created in the divine image and thus is loved unconditionally and is of unconditional value. Self-esteem will be discussed in chapter 1 as the first Biblical virtue and as a healthy habit that can free us from the pride-humility trap.

The second deadly sin is envy. Envy involves not simply wanting what someone else has but wishing that the other person did not have it. Like pride, it involves elevating the self against the other. The antidote prescribed for envy historically has been kindness or mercy. However, kindness or mercy can be erroneously interpreted as acceptance of a submissive role or status. This, of course, elevates the other over the self, the flip side of the same pathology. In contrast to both envy and submissiveness is the Biblical virtue of wisdom. People with wisdom know themselves and what their path is. They do not compare themselves to others, but follow their own path in life. Wisdom will be discussed in chapter 2.

The third deadly sin is anger that disconnects the self from others. This is the issue of *caaso* discussed previously. The prescribed antidote is peacefulness or patience. However, sometimes patience is not good, for it may be synonymous with passivity and can involve accepting an unjust situation, thus diminishing the self. The Bible speaks of times when righteous anger is called for. Chapter 3 presents the Biblical virtue of righteousness. Righteousness is not equivalent to a smug sense of self-righteousness, but rather to operating in a way that is moral and ethical. It does not connote playing God, but acting habitually in a Godly way.

The fourth deadly sin is lust, defined as an inordinate craving for the pleasures of the body. The other is turned into an object to satisfy one's own desires. This obviously elevates the self and dehumanizes the other. But the prescribed antidote of chastity is just as imbalanced. Chastity here seems to refer not simply to a sexual modesty, but to a turning away and negating of the physical. Here needs of the body and self are ignored. One squeamishly avoids any physical contact with the other. The Biblical gift deemphasizes both lust and chastity in favor of love. Biblical love is not just spiritual; it has a physical component as well. Yet physical desire is not mere lust, but an expression of love for the other, the highest relationship between people, and balances self and other. The Biblical conception of love is broader than that between a man and a woman. It includes love between friends, between parents and children, and of course, between the human being and God. As we will show in chapter 4, the Biblical virtue of love always integrates the physical and the spiritual. It is neither squeamish nor licentious.

Chapter 5 considers the sin of gluttony, which is defined as an inordinate desire to consume too much. It denotes excessive eating and drinking (*coso*) and reflects piggish behavior, which ignores the needs of others and concentrates only on the self. For the glutton, there is no beauty in food, there is just the food itself. There is no appreciation for the preparation or for the presentation of food, just the desire to consume. However, the historical antidote of abstinence is not much better. Here the self totally withdraws from things of the world, including the pleasure of good food, to prevent any exploitation of it. Such a stance can lead ultimately even to starvation. In contrast to both is the Biblical virtue of healthy appetite. A healthy person develops the habit of a healthy appetite; but that does not require descent into gluttony or a flip to the opposite extreme of total abstinence. A healthy person develops the habit of eating and drinking in a healthy manner.

Chapter 6 discusses the deadly sin of greed. It involves the desire for material wealth or gain, totally ignoring the realm of the spiritual. It is also called avarice or covetousness. Greed, like envy, ignores the other. The greedy person may become quite miserly and totally focus on the stockpiling of possessions, which, of course, will not bring happiness. The antidote to it may be just as imbalanced. Sometimes called liberality, the antidote reflects a wastefulness that runs the risk of ignoring one's material needs completely. Both extremes are denoted by *ciso* in the ancient Hebrew saying. The wasteful person is imprudent and may give everything away and wind up, like King Lear, destitute and dependent on the charity of others. The Biblical virtue avoids both the sin of greed and the antidote of wastefulness and emphasizes the habit of prudence, not a miserly thrift, but one that husbands one's resources to enable one to live with some modicum of independence while still allowing generosity to others. One has to have something in order to be generous.

Finally, the sin of sloth is discussed in chapter 7. Sloth is defined as the avoidance of physical or spiritual work. It is not mere laziness but dejection of the spirit. It is the complacency of people who neither care nor have any sense of what they want to do with their lives. This lack of commitment reflects a person who is lost, and does not indicate a strong sense of self or independence. The historical antidote has been called zeal or diligence. However, this can be equally unsatisfactory, resulting in workaholism—work for work's sake. This is no solution, subordinating the self into a deadening cacophony of meaningless activity. The Biblical virtue is quite different than either sloth or diligence. It is purpose. People with a sense of purpose see work as an expression of their deepest being. They do not find work to be alienating or unpleasantly burdensome, nor do they wander the world aimlessly. Their life has meaning as an expression of God's love for them.

Let us now turn to these seven Biblical virtues: seven habits of the good life.

Chapter One

Self-Esteem: An Escape from the Pride-Humility See-Saw

"So God created mankind in His own image, in the image of God He created him, male and female, he created them."

—Genesis 1:27

Pride has typically been viewed in western thought as a sin. Indeed, it is the first deadly sin. This is curious in itself. What is wrong with pride? Should a person not feel good about his/her accomplishments? A pride that becomes exaggerated into a pompous vanity is obviously not a positive trait. Prudentius's prescribed antidote to this sin is humility. True humility is certainly a great virtue and a means of balancing one's obsession with self with a concern for others. Often, however, it is misinterpreted as self-humiliation, self-flagellation and a sense of utter worthlessness. Do people need to castigate themselves all the time in order to avoid being pompous? Is the cure worse than the illness? Is the answer to self-glorification to be found in self-deprecation? Often lost in this antidote is a person's sense that he/she is created uniquely in God's image (Genesis1: 27). This should lead to the Biblical alternative of a genuine self-esteem, consisting of a healthy sense of self-worth that is grateful for the gifts one has been given, accompanied by a healthy modesty and ability to see oneself and others in perspective.

Consider Barbara, a forty-year-old woman constantly preening in the mirror. She spends an inordinate amount of time worrying about wrinkles and pounds that no one else seems to notice. She is consumed with herself, and has no time or energy for anyone else. Such a person can be

11

judged as vain or overly proud, and the antidote historically offered to her has been severe self-criticism.

However, a deeper analysis shows the flaw in this line of thinking. Barbara's self-absorption stems not from a genuine self-love but from insecurity. She is already too self-critical and the accentuation of her flaws will only worsen her self-esteem. The solution to Barbara's problem is neither more pride nor more humility, which represent two sides of the same coin, but rather a self-esteem based on a genuine sense of worth and on modesty. Self-worth is not the same as overweening pride nor is modesty the same as a self-effacing humility.

Consider a second example. Ralph is a gifted playwright. However, people are reluctant to invite him to their houses because he spends the entire evening talking about himself and his latest accomplishments. He shows no interest in anyone else, and people soon tire of him. Yet the prescribed antidote of humility may not provide a better solution. If Ralph becomes convinced that his plays are worthless, he is no better off than before, nor will that make him pleasant company.

Ralph's problem is that he does not have a genuine sense of worth. His air of superiority masks his inferiority, and concentration on his inadequacies only accentuates what he already feels. The solution for Ralph is to gain a genuine sense of self-esteem, where he can understand the real value of what he does and, at the same time, be attentive to others.

The problem in our thinking goes back to the classical Greek notion that *hubris* or an overweening pride is brought down by *Nemesis,* the god of destruction, leading to a person's downfall. The myth of Narcissus is a prime example of hubris that denotes an overweening pride. Narcissus is the offspring of a rape. A seer tells his mother he will live a long life provided he does not come to know himself. Because of what the seer told his mother, Narcissus is not allowed normal growth and development. Instead, he is sheltered from knowing his true self. Because he does not have authentic self-knowledge or self-esteem, Narcissus is totally absorbed in himself and is oblivious to others.

Narcissus seems filled with himself, but is really empty inside, and this emptiness leads him to reject would-be lovers of both sexes. One of the rejected suitors prays to the god Nemesis to punish Narcissus for his overweening hubris. Nemesis accomplishes this by causing Narcissus to become infatuated with his own image in a pond. Slowly realizing that he can never possess the image, he pines away until death overcomes him or, in another version of the story, stabs himself to death. Narcissus's inability to deal with his self-image leads him to a life of alienation and fleeing from reality, ultimately culminating in a wretched suicide.

The antidote prescribed for pride has been humility with a diminished self-consciousness and freedom from preoccupation with self. It involves a total rejection of any feeling of superiority that one may have due to ancestry, wealth, beauty, knowledge, athletic abilities, or achievements. This may be good in itself, but methods advocated to reach this state seem quite chilling to modern sensibilities.

Some thinkers prescribe a severe self-examination and self-criticism that focuses on one's deficiencies and mistakes, and even exaggerates them. The danger here is that we may so devalue ourselves that we feel constantly inferior, worthless and sinful. Sometimes, a seeming sense of inferiority may mask a superiority complex in some people, their very humility giving them a sense of secondary gain. And often the supposed humility may be totally false, concealing an avaricious and duplicitous personality, as exemplified in the literary figures of Dickens' Uriah Heep and Moliere's Tartuffe. Such humility does not seem likely to produce a more healthy personality than pride itself.

Indeed, pride and false humility can be seen as the two ends of a see-saw. Pride ignores the other at the expense of self. It appears as a sense of superiority but it masks an underlying sense of inferiority. False humility is often the opposite: a pretense of obsequiousness masking an underlying sense of superiority. What is missing in both of these tendencies is a sense of genuine self-esteem involving a healthy, grateful and modest sense of self-worth.

Consider the creation of Adam in the Garden of Eden in the Book of Genesis. Human existence, in a Biblical sense, is full of awe and wonderment at being created in God's image. Unlike Narcissus, who was condemned never to know his true self, God encourages his people "to be fruitful and multiply." Adam and Eve are blessed with opportunity, whereas Narcissus had wretched beginnings, and an even more miserable existence. The biggest difference was that Narcissus could not view himself as a special creation. He could not know the feeling that God had a special purpose for him, as Adam knew God had for him and Eve. Indeed, neither gods nor parents seemed to have any interest in Narcissus, despite his good looks.

Unlike Narcissus, who destroyed himself at his first challenge, Adam and Eve recovered from mistakes to produce the human race. They were still human beings created by God in God's own image. If they would look into a pond, they would see two images of God and understand that the world continues to have meaning. What they do and how well they fare is important to God, whose images they are. A person must remember, though it is sometimes hard to do, that he or she is special to God and that God did not commit a foolish mistake in creating this unique human being. Narcissus looked into the pool and saw nothing of this, only an alienated self. Narcissus was empty inside, he had no inner resources, nor did he have a God to help him recover from his mistakes. He does not see the image of God but only his own. He was finally undone by a fruitless attempt to unite with his own image.

Adam and Eve and their descendants can go on, pursuing the highest goals and having wonderful lives despite setbacks, precisely because they need never forget the fact that they are images of God, that they are important and that they have God's unconditional blessing and love.

The idea that a person is worth something no matter how sad the family background or personal mistakes cannot be emphasized enough and is stressed in Psalms 27:10. "Even though my father and mother abandon me, the Lord will take me in." Second, God Himself teaches Adam about the world (Gen. 2:19–20). Third, God gives Adam a mate because He knows it is not good for man to be alone. Finally, Adam is forbidden to enmesh himself in illusory knowledge (Gen. 2:17) because it obscures his fundamental relationship with God and his search after real understanding and acceptance of self and of the world. Authentic self-esteem allows us to avoid the traps of both pride and humility. A realistic sense of self-worth helps one to deal with all situations in a more positive and effective way.

The stories of Narcissus and Adam illustrate the importance of a genuine self-esteem and its effects on how one lives the rest of one's life. Adam, because of encouragement from God, grows to be a great man. Adam foregoes the destructiveness experienced by Narcissus because he has a genuine self-esteem. The fact that God is in Adam's life and available to both Adam and Eve in Eden produces a fulfilling self-image that pushes them to great achievements.

Adam and Eve know they are worth something because they are created in God's image. They are not filled with hubris, but neither do they fall to a nemesis. They do not need the antidote of the sort of false humility that is merely an obsession with their own imperfections. Self-esteem is central to mental health. Without a healthy self-esteem, an individual typically is unable to succeed in either love or work.

In love, an individual may be afraid to develop and express unique, even idiosyncratic aspects of his/her own personality for fear of being rejected by others. Instead he will disguise more personal expressions of his own self under the mask of social convention. For example, an individual with low self-esteem may appear stiff and pompous. In work, too, the individual may be afraid to express his or her own ideas and, thus, one's own creativity, because of fear of criticism and the need for approval. Being afraid to be different inhibits what might be a person's most valuable contributions. One may be unable to utilize special gifts and may be paralyzed by imperfections or disabilities.

Many people never develop a healthy self-esteem, and indeed its development demands persistence and understanding of some concepts that people find difficult to accept. In Biblical terms, one must begin by accepting the very fundamental premise that people are created by God and that God does not make mistakes. It would be a foolish and false modesty for a person to feel that God had blundered or mixed the wrong ingredients in making him or her. Every human being is created unique and important and with the opportunity and indeed the obligation to do his or her best.

Each human being is created uniquely in God's own image. One need not compare oneself to another. Individuals should not feel guilty about talents or gifts with which God has blessed them. Instead, one should thank God for the gifts and use them in the best ways possible. For a person to act as though he does not have a gift or talent that he in fact does have is highly counterproductive and may result from or lead to low self-esteem.

Let us return to Barbara who, like Narcissus, is constantly preening in the mirror. She is obsessed with outer manifestations of beauty because she is alienated, like Narcissus, from authentic self-knowledge. To the extent that she genuinely comes to know herself, she will put herself in touch with her inner beauty, reflecting her sense that she has been created in God's own image. Barbara will not be consumed like Narcissus was, with her reflection in the mirror. Rather, her beauty will shine out from her countenance and she will develop relationships with people around her. She will be modest, but not overly self-critical, nor will she hide her abilities. Rather, she will see her abilities as God-given gifts and she will feel a responsibility and joy to develop them to help improve the world.

Consider the Biblical story of Samson and Delilah. The Philistines of that era were great warriors and they dominated the neighboring people of Israel. God sent Samson to aid the Israelites in their fight against the Philistines, who had far superior weapons. Samson was not simply a rippling mass of muscle. He may not have been very big at all. His special God-given strength was to be used to defend his people. However, Samson also had an occasional weakness for women, which would eventually lead to his destruction.

Samson was to drink no wine, to avoid ritual impurities, and was never to cut his hair as a physical sign on his head that he was to be God's sacred instrument for overthrowing the Philistines. Samson's strength was his special gift from God and should have created in him a genuine sense of self-esteem that would be used for God's purposes. However, Samson did not value this special gift enough. He was undone by his susceptibility to feminine charms and did not pay sufficient attention to his God-given gift. The Philistine leaders bribed his wife Delilah to learn the secret of Samson's prowess. Delilah learned his secret and used it against him, cutting his hair while he was sleeping. Bereft of his strength, Samson was easy prey for the Philistines, who blinded him and sent him to a prison. "Samson followed his eyes; therefore the Philistines gouged them out" (*Talmud, Sota* 9b).

Samson's weakness in following his eyes led him to yield to Delilah and finally to lose both his eyes and his special strength as well. There was no magic in Samson's hair, no elixir of superhuman strength. Rather, God was displeased that Samson was so careless about the main sign of his special mission. He failed to treasure God's special gift to him and was punished for being so careless. Yet Samson's mission did not fail completely. Even in his blindness, he would strike one more smashing blow that would cow the Philistines for years, when he pulled down the pillars of the temple of Dagon in Gaza and destroyed thousands of enemies in a moment.

This story demonstrates that a human being must not dissipate his or her special God-given talents. We are, each of us, obliged to use them in a constructive way. Let us return to the case of the playwright, Ralph, discussed earlier. To the extent that Ralph comes to see his literary talents as a gift from God, he will display a natural modesty. He will not deny or evade his gifts, or, like Samson, do things to dissipate them. On the other hand, he will not need to act pompously, boring everyone around him by talking incessantly about his achievements

When Ralph realizes that his gifts as a playwright are God-given, he will not need to display an overbearing sense of superiority or feel overly susceptible to criticism. Ralph does not need to feel worthless as an antidote against overweening pride.

Unlike Greek tragedy, the Bible portrays human beings as brought to destruction not through an arbitrary decree of fate or of the gods but through their own willfulness. Samson brought about his own downfall. He had a special gift and the free will to make good use of it. In one sense, he succeeded greatly for he accomplished the protection of his people. Yet he also "went after his eyes" and diminished the sanctity of his life and work. It is not enough for a person merely to be gifted. He must learn to use these gifts in a healthy way for himself and others and must work against being stultified by them.

Essential to mental health is the capacity of a person to accept talents as God-given and to use them in a constructive way. This means neither to seek self-aggrandizement through them, nor to exhibit a false pride. Denying or ignoring one's unique gifts and mission is a false humility. Rather, a person with a healthy self-esteem will acknowledge his unique gifts and use them positively and modestly as part of a purpose and context larger than himself.

Let us turn to the very well-known story of David and Goliath. It is more than the tale of the victory of a dauntless young lad against a giant warrior. It is also a confrontation between two views of strength—the Hebrew Bible's and that of the Philistine warrior-hero. A Philistine army invaded Israel, and King Saul gathered his soldiers to meet them. As the two armies faced each other, the giant Goliath stepped forth from his own ranks to challenge an Israelite champion to single combat. He and his armament were huge and impressive. Goliath also used verbal abuse to cower and unnerve the Israelites. "I scorn the ranks of Israel. The Israelites are cowards. If no one comes voluntarily, let them pick one man to face me" (I Sam. 17:8).

Saul and his army were overwhelmed with fear, no one wanting to step forward to face the giant. David, however, did not fall into Goliath's trap. He recognized that Goliath was entrapped by his own pride. David had a genuine self-esteem and offered to fight the giant. King Saul did not understand: "You cannot go to fight against this Philistine. For you are an inexperienced lad and he is a warrior trained from youth" (I Sam.17:33).

David replied with a story of how he slew a bear and a lion that had attacked his sheep: "And this uncircumcised Philistine is like one of them, for he has scorned the ranks of the living God" (17:34–36). He convinced Saul that God was with him, and Saul consented to allow David to fight Goliath. "And Saul said to David, 'Go and God be with you.'" (17:37).

David fought with the assurance of great faith—that if a person did what is right, then he could be sure that God would be pleased. How did David know that he could win against this warrior who had crushed the Israelite army with words? Was he delusional? Was he relying on a miracle? David believed in miracles. Yet here, David did not seem to have felt that there was a need for one. He understood something that the other Israelites had forgotten—the importance of the mental and the spiritual in warfare. He seemed to have correctly sized up the inflated ego of Goliath whose spirit could not match his muscles.

David picked up five stones and approached the Philistine. Goliath seemed taken aback, confused and certainly insulted. "Am I a dog that you come to me with sticks?"(17:43). David must have sensed Goliath's inner weakness. Like many macho bullies and like the typical Homeric hero, Goliath had, in fact, a very poor self-image. David understood too that Goliath found it difficult to move under the heavy armor.

David's reply was straightforward and sure. He came in God's name and would slay Goliath. He was acting on a very intelligent plan and knew exactly what he was doing, killing Goliath with one slung stone while running straight for the Philistine army. David acted with confidence and self-esteem, knowing that God was with him at all times, and that the winning of a war is surely in God's hands.

There is much more to the story than a young shepherd versus a skilled and seasoned warrior. David was not a bully, as was Goliath; he did not need to cast verbal insults or use a sense of false pride to win. Instead, David had a relationship with God and a deep feeling for his own people, and his self-concept was in good shape. He was modest but not paralyzed by self-humiliation disguised as humility. He felt obligated to apply his God-given gifts to defend his people. And David was realistic as well, believing that with the help of God, he could defeat Goliath and save the Israelites. David's modesty resulted from a healthy self-esteem.

Sometimes people feel that they have no significant strengths in their personality. They feel unworthy of being loved and incapable of serious work. It is especially surprising that often these very people have a great deal going for them. They may be sensitive, kind, intelligent, resourceful and likable. Why do they discount all these attributes and focus instead on their limitations? Perhaps, following the attitudes in society, they mistakenly see sensitivity as weak, kindness as foolish, intelligence as useless, and resourcefulness as tricky. They may admit to being likable but deny that there is any good reason for anyone to like them. It is the "If they only knew" syndrome. This sense of mistaken humility may be a consequence of non-constructive parental criticism of any imperfection of the person when he/she was a child.

The Bible teaches us to accurately assess both our strengths and weaknesses. Such an approach is necessary to make us feel good about attributes we failed to acknowledge in ourselves. David cannot beat Goliath at his own game. He must go with his own strength to succeed. Such an awareness of one's strengths and weaknesses is essential for an individual to cope with the opportunities and setbacks of life and to convert potential disasters into triumphs.

Low self-esteem resembles modesty only in a superficial and distorted way. True modesty demands a realistic insight into one's self and a proper respect for God and for people. This is not the same as humility, at least the wrong kind of humility. True modesty is based on a genuine self-esteem. It involves recognizing the limitations of mortal human power and control while at the same time using the abilities that one does have. It does not mean thinking that one is slow-witted when he is, in fact, very bright or thinking one is homely when he is, in fact, of pleasing appearance. If one is a great scholar, she should acknowledge that fact and use

Chapter 1

her learning well. She should not insist on seeing herself as unlearned nor should she use her talents to elevate herself above other people. To think one is less than one is amounts to demeaning God's creation and belittles the divine image in which humankind was created. People often seek to build themselves up by honors or by accomplishments—by piling up wealth, publishing their writings or winning ball games. In fact, no accomplishment, no matter how great or heroic, can produce self-esteem. It may produce short-term satisfaction or pride. However, true self-esteem must be based on the belief that one is created by a loving God.

Consider the Biblical story of the meeting of Elisha, the Israelite prophet and Naaman, the powerful Syrian general. Naaman was the glorious and highly honored commander of the armies of the warlike King Ben Hadad of Aram (Syria). Yet, along with all this, he was afflicted by a disease, perhaps leprosy, which made him miserable. The first hint of hope for Naaman and the first sense, as well, of an area of life not subject to his own sort of power came in a piece of advice from a little Israelite girl who had been captured in a Syrian raid into Israel. "Let my master entreat of the prophet in Samaria. He will recover him from his leprosy." (2 Kings 5:2–3).

Naaman proceeded with his large retinue of horses and riders and his great display of wealth and power, and he alighted before the door of Elisha's modest home. Elisha would not even step out of his home to talk to Naaman. Elisha was not behaving this way out of rudeness or inhospitability but out of a need to demonstrate that he rejected the superficiality and emptiness of Naaman's world. He would not meet Naaman on Naaman's terms but only on his own. Instead the prophet sent a message whose deeper meaning did not become clear until later. "Go and wash seven times in the Jordan, and your skin will be restored and healed" (5:10). Elisha did not address the general by his accustomed titles. He merely issued a seemingly frivolous command, which it turned out was not frivolous at all.

Naaman was upset and angered. He had expected the prophet to behave in a pompous manner, to use magic, and above all to respect Naaman's exalted position. Elisha did none of these things. He was not playing the game by Naaman's rules, was not assuming his expected role nor allowing Naaman his accustomed status. Namaan needed to learn that he was to live without all his arrogant trappings and attitudes. He needed to live in modesty, not in pride. Naaman came out both wiser and stronger. It is not any magical power of the river that heals and elevates man, but his learning the importance of realism and true humility. Naaman was cured both of his illness and of his illusions. Elisha removed Naaman's misconceptions gently but firmly, and the hope of a more meaningful life awaited him.

Many psychological problems manifest themselves in physical ailments. A child from an overbearing family finds it difficult to breathe and develops an asthmatic condition. Treatment reveals that as the child's parents back off, the child's asthmatic problems diminish. Another patient is referred to a therapist by a rheumatologist because of back problems resulting from poor posture. It becomes clear in the process of therapy that the patient finds it difficult to stand up for himself in a healthy way. He either walks bent over or thrusts his body forward aggressively. As the patient learns to be properly assertive rather than submissive or domineering, his body posture improves and his back pains subside. He escapes living with a false pride or inappropriate humility and learns genuine modesty and healthy self-esteem. An individual must learn the emptiness of external display. A simple approach can offer an access to wisdom obscured by overly complicated solutions, which themselves are products of a defensive posture towards life.

Chapter Two

Wisdom: An Escape from the Envy-Submissiveness See-Saw

"And God said to him [Solomon] . . . lo, I have given thee a wise and understanding heart."

—I Kings 3:11–12

Envy has been seen as a major cause of human problems. It emerges typically from a sense of loss and threat we feel when someone else has something that we do not. Envy may generate hatred for the other or the desire to take away his coveted possession. Sometimes it may even provoke a drive to hurt or destroy. Prudentius has offered the antidote of kindness, which is itself commendable, and may imply a genuine concern for others. However, kindness can sometimes be confused with submissiveness, which can reflect an unwarranted acceptance of one's inferior status. A person may accept less pay or less recognition for his or her accomplishments because he/she does not feel worthy of recognition. The person may appear to be "kind," but his kindness may mask an underlying retreat from life itself.

Biblical thought is not opposed to a person trying to achieve goals. Indeed, it is healthy for a person to want to improve himself and his lot. But it is important for a person to pursue goals that fit him or her and not pursue goals that don't. This distinction requires wisdom and a knowledge of who one is. This is not an abstract knowledge but a personal knowledge. Significantly, this personal knowledge is denied to Narcissus in the Greek myth (Ovid, *The Metamorphosis*, 30: 347–359). He will live a long life only if he does not come to know himself. Yet it is exactly this self-knowledge that is essential for avoiding the pitfalls of both envy and submissiveness that occur when we lack the self-knowledge to know what is rightfully ours and what is not ours.

Personal wisdom involves knowing who we are and who we are not, what our talents and weaknesses are and what they are not. Personal wisdom is essential to knowing what to accept and what not to accept, and when to act and when not to act. Reinhold Neibuhr says this very well in his serenity prayer: "God grant me the serenity to accept the things I cannot change, courage to change the things I can, and wisdom to know the difference." To not accept what should be accepted leads to envy. To accept what should not be accepted leads to submissiveness. Wisdom is essential to avoid both ends of the see-saw. It tells us when it is appropriate to accept something and when it is appropriate instead to seek to change it.

Helen has worked in an import office for a number of years. She is hardworking and knows her field well, especially the manufacturing of textiles in India. A shy person, Helen has not mixed easily with others in her office. Over the course of time, she finds that she has been consistently passed over for promotions, raises and other perks which have been given to workers who were less talented and devoted than she.

One of these people is Helen's friend Betty. How should Helen react? Should she be envious of Betty? This is not a constructive solution, as these feelings will undermine their friendship. Helen will be bitter and resentful toward any good fortune that may come Betty's way. On the other hand, it is not good for Helen to accept her inferior status as appropriate and well-deserved, as Prudentius's solution of liberality implies. Prudentius seems to advocate that Helen defend herself against her feelings of powerlessness to change by seeing herself as inferior to Betty in achievements but superior morally. Yet this solution actually amounts to self-belittlement in moral dress.

Neither envy nor self-belittlement will serve Helen well. The first alternative will leave her bitter and angry, the second will leave her feeling beaten and inferior. We would recommend a truly Biblical solution: genuine self-knowledge, which can help enable her to accurately understand and assess her own abilities as compared to those of Betty and others in the office.

Helen can ask for a review of her work with her supervisor. With this information, she can more accurately assess her future in this office and determine her own course of action: whether to try to improve her social skills in the office or to look for another job and a context where her talents will be more appreciated. This solution will leave Helen feeling neither aggravated nor unworthy.

How does one become wise? Is it something that we can learn in school, from books, from parents? America has entered what may be called a crisis of wisdom. Major newspapers regularly print articles focusing on the problems in our schools at every level. Our students are falling behind in mathematics and science, and the students at major universities seem to have no knowledge of important and basic historical facts. The way some people answer Jay Leno's questions regarding history and geography is saddening as well as funny: adults who don't believe there is a North Pole or who think that the Vietnamese War was fought in Korea. Despite all sorts of testing, and the availability of new instructional technology including the internet, we seem to be losing the battle of the schools.

Perhaps part of the problem is the gap between knowledge and wisdom. One can amass much knowledge of science or history, can learn ten languages and be a computer whiz, and still be very unhappy. The reason is that he or she has never in fact gained wisdom from all this knowledge. Of what value is the knowledge if the person never can use it to benefit others or oneself? Nuclear power is wonderful, but what if it falls into the hands of terrorists? People or nations may know how to do something without actually knowing whether, when or why it should or should not be done.

Learning requires that a person have enough trust in a teacher, an author, or a parent to be a student or an apprentice. It is wonderful if one can trust that the authority really does want one to gain autonomy and independence. But what if the authority does not want the student to become autonomous and tries to block him by withholding information or providing confusing, misleading or false information?

In the Greek myth of Prometheus and Pandora, for example, Prometheus steals fire from Zeus to give to man. Zeus counters by sending the first woman, Pandora, as a punishment to man. Although Pandora is beautiful and talented, she has low morals. She ultimately opens the famous box which Zeus gave her, unleashing all the evils it contained upon the world, leaving only hope locked up inside and unavailable. We will discuss the negative light this story casts on women in chapter 4. Here we raise the question as to why Zeus should begrudge man something so entirely essential as fire. It is needed for heat and light. It separates the clearing from the wilderness, and the domestic from the wild. The rays of light provide a safe haven against the wild creatures of the darkness. Fire provides heat to make weapons to hunt, and utensils to cook the product of the hunt. It allows the making of wheels, which greatly facilitate travel. So why should Zeus deny people this knowledge? One can only conclude that Zeus, selfish and capricious as always, cares little for people and wants to keep them subservient. *It is clear that classical man must rebel against Zeus to obtain knowledge.*

This tendency can be seen in the curious ambivalence toward wisdom and self-knowledge displayed in Greek and world literature. On the one hand, knowledge in the Greek world is turned into a contest, much like the TV quiz programs. Debates similarly reward flashy and detached intellectual sophistry rather than true wisdom emerging from genuine knowledge of self and others. Each person is envious of the others and is driven to defeat them. On the other hand, the ancient Oracle at Delphi issued the dictum "Know thyself," by which it meant knowing one's place. This directive seems to evoke a tendency toward submissiveness.

Narcissus is promised a long life providing "he does not come to know himself." This negative view of self-knowledge may emerge from the impossible dilemmas or Hobson's choices (having two unsatisfactory possibilities to choose from, but having to choose one or the other) facing many of literature's heroic figures. They often must choose between envy and submissiveness. Wisdom is not really an ally when all of the several possible solutions are self-destructive. Indeed, Jocasta says this directly to her son/husband Oedipus, trying to stop his search for his parentage that will lead to his destruction: "Ill-fated one! May thou never come to know who thou art!" (Oedipus Rex l. 1077–78)

The Bible, in contrast, greatly approves of our having knowledge and offers a view of how wisdom can make knowledge a blessing and not a curse. Books like Proverbs and Ecclesiastes have a great deal to say on the topic. Wisdom is not simply the accumulation of knowledge and is not intended to foster envy or submissiveness, but to help a person live a full and meaningful life. Consider the ringing Biblical dictum: "The beginning of wisdom is reverence for God" (Psalms 111:10). This same idea appears in Proverbs 1:7, 2:6, 4:7, 9:10; Psalms 1:11, 25; Job 28:11; and Proverbs 2:6.

What does this mean? The Biblical God is not Zeus. He is not selfish and capricious. To understand this, we must remember that God created people in an act of unconditional love. He does not wish to keep them subservient but to have them grow in wisdom. This wisdom will come from working at and understanding God's teaching and God's world. God taught Adam all about the animals and had Adam assign them names. He gave man in Eden all the resources and knowledge that he needs to live a productive life, and He provided Adam with a companion, Eve. However, God forbade Adam and Eve to eat of the tree of knowledge of good and evil.

In one of Scripture's most fascinating stories, the serpent persuades Eve to disobey God and eat of the tree, offering the promise to Eve "of being as God, knowing good and evil" (Gen: 3:5). The deceptiveness of the serpent is revealed in his mischaracterization of God. The Biblical God does not merely "know good and evil." He determines what is good and what is evil. In this story, God is prohibiting pseudo-wisdom and knowledge that is cut off from the divine plan, that comes magically from a fruit, and that will mislead man into nothing but self-centeredness. Biblical man does not need to rebel against the Biblical God to acquire knowledge, for this God is not blocking man by depriving him of fire (Genesis Rabbah 11:2) the way Zeus does. Rather, the God of the Bible has already given Adam everything he needs to learn and to thrive. (Gen. 1:29). The serpent is offering the promise of a false wisdom which will block rather than facilitate self-knowledge.

The Biblical idea of knowledge is expressed in the knowledge that Adam has of Eve. It is a personal knowledge, a knowledge that is both sexual and spiritual, a relational knowledge that a man has of a woman, and that allows procreation and the continuation of the species. It is real rather than meaningless knowledge and allows fulfillment of the Biblical commandment: "Be fruitful, and multiply" (Gen. 1:28). "And Adam *knew* Eve his wife, and she conceived" (Gen. 4:1). This knowledge, unlike that offered by the serpent, is in reverence of God and His plan. This wisdom is essential in overcoming the polarities of envy and submissiveness.

A person does not have to be Biblically religious to realize the limitations of his or her own knowledge. One simply must know that he or she does not and cannot know everything by oneself. This is the realization that life has mysteries beyond normal human understanding. One of the greatest of Greek thinkers, Socrates himself, whom many consider to be the founder of the science of philosophy as we know it today, seemed to understand this. The god Apollo, speaking through the Oracle at Delphi, had pronounced Socrates to be the wisest of all men. Socrates did not know what his statement meant and began an endeavor to discover why that statement was so: why he was the wisest of all men. Inquiring of many people—poets, tradesmen, politicians and so on, Socrates found that each of the men considered himself to be wise in that he knew his own field. Socrates learned that there was one thing he knew that none of the others knew: no one is truly wise, and true wisdom belongs to the gods alone.

This seems to be not unlike the Biblical dictum, cited above, that wisdom begins with reverence for God. However, the Bible adds an important new level to the human yearning for wisdom. Consider Solomon, who was still young and awed by the tasks facing him when he succeeded his father David as king of Israel (I Kings 3:7–8). "I am a young lad and I do not know how to go and come. And Your servant is in the midst of Your people whom You have chosen, a great people whose multitude can not be numbered or counted." When God told Solomon to ask for what he wanted most, the young king asked for "a heart to hear and to judge Your people, to understand good from evil" (3:9). Inexperienced as he was, Solomon was already wise enough to know that he could rule well only with wisdom and with faith in God.

There are certainly points in common in these accounts of two brilliant men, the Greek philosopher and the King of Israel. Both sought and attained great wisdom. However, the two approaches to wisdom show significant differences. Socrates never dealt directly with Apollo. While Apollo hinted at the mission of seeking wisdom, he actually gave Socrates no help and did not teach him. What Apollo did was give Socrates a task or labor much like Hera gave Heracles a series of different labors. And what was the essence of Socrates's wisdom? Only to know how much he does not know. The Oracle at Delphi greeted visitors to the shrine similarly with the inscription over the entrance, "Know Thyself," which essentially means "Know your place, and do not think much of yourself."

The oracle is prescribing submissiveness as the antidote to envy. It is noteworthy that Apollo never spoke to Socrates directly. This message came through the oracle. Other messages later came, said Socrates, from a daimon, a sort of spirit that could function as an intermediary between gods and men, but was itself less than a god.

Solomon, in contrast, felt close enough to God to ask directly for the gift of the virtue of wisdom. Solomon's purpose and direction began with a love of God: "And Solomon loved God" (3:3). God promised great wisdom to Solomon and assured him of material support as well—"wealth and honor which no man ever had like you among kings" (3:13). Solomon was very wise not only in recognizing his own limitations and God's greatness and wisdom but also in many areas of knowledge. When God appeared to the young Solomon in a dream and asked him, "What shall I give you?" (I Kings 3:5), Solomon gave a thoughtful answer. He realized that he was young and lacked the experience to make wise decisions. He realized he did not know "how to go out or come in" (3:7). Give your servant "a heart that hears," he prayed, so that he can lead the people and decide between what is good and what is bad (3: 9). God approved of Solomon's request. He would grant to Solomon more wisdom than to any other man (3:12). Solomon's work will be to use his gifts to follow God's teachings (3:14).

A great test of Solomon's practical wisdom would come soon in his encounter with two harlots who lived in the same house. As it happened, they had each given birth to a son within three days of each other. The first woman claimed that the child of the second had died during the night and that the other had switched babies, taking the living one for herself (3:16–21). The second woman replied, "No, for my son is the living and your son is the dead." And the first woman said, "No, for yours is the dead and mine is the living." There were neither witnesses to the event nor any other proofs, and to Solomon's courtiers the case must have seemed impossible to resolve.

Solomon, in fact, by his mental keenness and spiritual openness had already figured out which child belonged to which mother. First, Solomon very carefully repeated the statements of the two women: "And the king said, 'This one says, "This is my son that liveth, and your son is the dead." And the other says, "No, but your son is the dead, and mine is the living"'" (3:23). The false mother was acting out of envy, and seemed to cow the true mother into submissiveness.

By paying close attention to what the women said, Solomon avoided both polarities and employed a personal wisdom to catch the fact that one woman consistently mentioned the living child first. The other woman consistently mentioned the dead child first, where she should have answered, "No, mine is the living and yours is the dead." Solomon understood that the mother mentioning the living child first was the mother of the living child and the mother mentioning the dead child first was the mother of the dead child.

However, Solomon grasped that an even greater problem of demonstrating this to everyone's satisfaction still remained so that later there could be no doubt as to the mother. Solomon called for a sword to cut the living child in half, counting on the women's reactions to reveal before everyone who the real mother was. (3:24–25) The false claimant advanced a very legitimate argument in favor of his death. "He won't be mine and he won't be yours" (3:26). This response is the essence of envy. The false claimant is willing to kill the child rather than let him live with the true mother. The true mother, of course, could not bear to see the child killed and begged that instead he be allowed to live even as the other woman's son.

Nevertheless, the false claimant's response made clear that the fact that she always mentioned "your dead child" before "my living child" was no coincidence, and that in her grief over her own loss, she wanted the real mother to suffer the loss of her child, too. She was filled with envy, trying to take something that was not hers. Solomon had demonstrated that his deduction (in 3:23) was absolutely correct, and he handed the child to the true mother. Not only had Solomon's wisdom solved a seemingly insoluble problem, but it had sliced right through the potential Hobson's dilemma by demonstrating to all and perhaps to himself as well that his judgment had been correct. The judgment helped to establish Solomon's reputation for wisdom and perceptiveness.

This story illustrates the way in which a person may often know intuitively the answer to a vexing problem. Yet one must find some acceptable way of demonstrating the truth of those inner instincts. It is not always clear whether the demonstration is to oneself or to others. However, in either case, a public event may often demonstrate rather than determine the correctness of a decision. Implicit knowledge must be integrated with explicit demonstration to complete many difficult decisions. It is important to learn that it is often not enough merely to be right. One must sometimes also be able to demonstrate clearly to others and indeed to oneself that his or her judgment is correct. The act of working and the basis by which the person may know the truth can serve as a demonstration for others.

This story is very significant for human psychology. An individual may, like Socrates, be intelligent enough to realize the limitations of human wisdom. His intellect can take him only so far—and then he seems to have reached a brick wall. Like Socrates, the person may despair—feeling that true wisdom belongs only to the gods—and that the entire human enterprise of acquiring knowledge is futile and even tragic.

Alternatively, one may react like Solomon, realizing that his own intellect can take him only so far, but that God will help him understand. Such an individual will listen to the wisdom of his heart and to his intuitions, as well as to the wisdom of others, understanding that wisdom is not of the intellect alone but of his entire being. An individual should also realize that the intellect need not manifest itself in rebellion toward the emotional life, but should be in harmony with it. It is God who will help us on our path and not the snake in the Garden of Eden.

Knowledge, wealth and physical well-being are all part of God's bounty to humanity and all worth working for. However, they must be pursued in the context of a wisdom that emerges from healthy self-knowledge. Without healthy self-knowledge, ambition can descend to arrogance, greed, or lust for power. I Kings 11:26 tells of the career of Jeroboam, whose great drive and talent were thrown off track by his insatiable envy.

King Solomon saw in Jeroboam special abilities and appointed him to a high post in the government. All people need some bit of self-confidence, but Jeroboam seemed to be arrogant to a fault and did not really know himself. He seems to have been obsessed with envy toward King David and his descendants. These deficiencies in wisdom became evident upon the splitting of the kingdom of Israel after Solomon's death into the kingdoms of Judah (including the site of the holy temple in Jerusalem) in the south and Israel in the north. Jeroboam ruled the kingdom of Israel while Solomon's son ruled the kingdom of Judah. Jeroboam attempted to de-legitimize Jerusalem by setting up new religious centers in Dan and Bethel within his kingdom and even erecting statues of golden calves.

He did this solely to play out his ambition for power. He could have been a very great leader of an Israelite kingdom. Instead, his envy led him to lose all that the Lord had meant for him and his family. Two years after his own death, Jeroboam's successor and his entire family were murdered by his general, Baasha.

This story reflects the need for balance of the various forces in a person's life—the desire to succeed as an individual in the context of appreciating the other and the social context. A person must be supported in the undertaking to be all he/she can be, and psychological blocks that impede this progress must be removed. At the same time, the person must be helped to set appropriate goals—not to strive for something that is not good for him or her.

This distinction is delicate and requires wisdom. The person must be encouraged neither to under-reach nor to overreach, but to seek what suits his or her personal character and abilities. Ambition in the service of fulfilling one's potential must be encouraged, but this must be distinguished from mindless self-aggrandizement and perpetual discontent. Once again this requires wisdom and self-knowledge. No myth provides a better example of the importance of genuine self-knowledge than Oedipus. Oedipus's major problem is that he does not know who he is. Throughout this story, Oedipus is misled by maddening and misleading riddles. Soothsayers and oracles give him incomplete and tantalizing information. Rather than help him, the information leads him inexorably to his destruction. A case in point is the message of an oracle when Oedipus comes to manhood in Corinth, after being saved from death and adopted by the king and queen of Corinth. The oracle tells Oedipus that he is destined to kill his father and marry his mother, but neglects to tell him that the king and queen of Corinth are his adopted parents. If Oedipus knew this missing piece of information, he would have stayed in Corinth with his adopted parents and kept away from Thebes and his biological parents.

But Oedipus, like Narcissus, does not know his identity. Thinking that the king and queen of Corinth are his biological father and mother, and horrified at the words of the oracle, Oedipus flees back into Thebes precisely to avoid fulfilling the oracular prophecy. But, of course, unbeknownst to Oedipus, and left unsaid by the oracle, Oedipus's biological father and mother are in Thebes. Journeying to Thebes, Oedipus finds himself in a conflict on the road with a belligerent older man who attacks him. In self-defense, Oedipus kills him, not realizing that the man is Laius, his biological father. Later he solves the aging riddle of the Sphinx: "What walks on four legs in the morning, two legs in the afternoon, and three legs in the evening?" Oedipus answers "man," accepting a cyclical or decremental theory of human development and aging, which views the older person as a child, and the end of life as no different than the beginning. For many psychological qualities, this view is clearly not true and life is far more linear. For example, wisdom should increase with age for a person who is living in a healthy manner. Oedipus is in a prototypical Hobson's choice, damned if he does and damned if he doesn't. If he does not answer the riddle of the Sphinx with the cyclical response, he will be devoured by the Sphinx. By answering "man," however, and accepting the cyclical view of human development, he blurs the demarcation line between the generations which forbids incest. If the older person is like a baby, then what is a parent and what is a child? Oedipus is "rewarded" by being given the widowed Jocasta to marry, not realizing that she is his biological mother and thus fulfilling the prophecy of the oracle, and providing the Sphinx posthumously with its greatest victory. Because of the maddening riddles, incomplete information and lack of knowledge regarding his own identity, the attempt of Oedipus to avoid his fate only tends to further bring it about.

Later in the narrative, Oedipus continues to act nobly, seeking out the murderer of King Laius in order to save Thebes from divine punishment. But learning that he himself is the murderer leads inexorably to the ruination of his own life and his family's. No wonder his mother-wife Jocasta attempts to stop Oedipus's search, crying "What good is wisdom if it does not benefit the wise?" Jocasta is convinced that Oedipus's learning of his true identity will lead to his destruction. Once again the Greek negative attitude toward self-knowledge manifests itself. Knowing your identity can destroy you.

Biblical man does not have this ambivalence. God had commanded people to study and acquire knowledge and to pass this on to their children in the most thorough manner—"And you shall teach your children diligently" (Deut. 6:7). This is a great responsibility, but God offers loving help. God Himself began the chain of transmission by personally giving the Ten Commandments to the Israelites at Sinai and many more laws and ideas as well during the forty years in the wilderness. And even earlier, God had taught Adam in the Garden of Eden all about nature and science (Gen. 2:19–20). Certainly a wise person ought to be humble. However, there is more to wisdom than humility, and God gives of His own wisdom and creativity to humanity and helps and supports them in their searching and development.

For Biblical people, God is the teacher of wisdom. God starts by teaching Adam all about the animals and having him give them names. He intervenes frequently to help people. He presents the Ten Commandments to the Israelites. The idea of a personal relationship with a loving and omniscient God was essentially unknown in the Hellenic world. Nor did the Greeks have a concept of divinely revealed knowledge. There could be soothsaying or prophecy of a sort, but no instruction. No Greek deity could have given the Ten Commandments nor would he/she have taught Greeks as the Biblical God taught Moses and the prophets.

God wants people to learn and to grow in wisdom. This wisdom will come from working and understanding God's teaching and God's world. It will not come from a quick fix or eating fruit from a magic tree as a serpent promised and as Adam and Eve seemed temporarily to believe.

In the Bible's view the most important wisdom is that God teaches the difference between right and wrong. The Book of Proverbs offers many scenarios where people make wrong decisions because they lack wisdom. A young man with some money in his pocket may find himself tempted by momentary indulgences. Adolescents are particularly prone to acting on whim, not wisdom. Yet, even several recent presidents of the United States did not avoid unwise decisions that affected both their personal and political lives.

Knowledge is wonderful, but knowledge alone does not make a person wise or good. Learned scientists have often used their knowledge to support evil governments and evil causes, like the scientists of the Third Reich or the modern terrorists. Culture, too, is wonderful, but there have been famous artists and professors who have been miserable human beings.

Consider the debate today regarding reproductive cloning. Science has advanced to the point where it may be possible for a person to duplicate himself without union between a man and a woman. But should we allow this procedure to occur or will it introduce all sorts of biological and ethical disasters? The Greek and Biblical stories of the repopulation of the world after the great flood speak exactly to this point. In the Greek account, Deucalion throws stones over his shoulder and they become men and Pyrrha throws stones over her shoulder and they become women (Apollodorus 1.7:2). In the Biblical story, males and female mate to repopulate the earth according to God's design. The Greek procedure of repopulation is exactly what some advocates of reproductive cloning advocate to this day. It certainly runs counter to the plan attributed to the Biblical God. Cloning for reproductive purposes certainly depends on a knowledge base. However, it is difficult to say if it is a wise procedure.

The Bible firmly believes that true wisdom begins with reverence of God. And it is indeed a gift from God. We must understand that wisdom is good and that God wants us to grow in wisdom. There is no sense that knowledge or wisdom, in itself, is forbidden or harmful for people. However, knowledge used immorally is harmful.

The Bible tells the story of Balaam, a brilliant man and a prophet, but thoroughly unscrupulous. He was willing to struggle with God to cast magical curses to harm the Israelites both for his own pleasure and for pay (Num. 22.2f.). Clearly, knowledge and talent alone do not make a person worthy or make his life valuable. It is what he does with this knowledge. It must be used to fulfill God's purposes and to know one's calling in life. Thus a person can avoid the twin pitfalls of envy and submissiveness the latter masquerading as misplaced kindness.

Chapter Three

Righteousness: An Escape from the Anger-Passivity See-Saw

"And it came to pass, as soon as he [Moses] came near the camp, that he saw the calf and the dancing, and Moses' anger burned and he threw the tablets out of his hands, and broke them at the foot of the mountains."

—Exodus 32:19

Anger has been seen by many social philosophers as the most dangerous of all the deadly sins, inextricably linked to sins like pride and envy, as well as to hatred and desire for revenge. It can be gratuitous and excessive, and is sometimes foisted on an innocent bystander. No wonder the issue of how a person handles his *caaso* (anger) is emphasized in the Hebrew saying with which we opened this book.

Prudentius has offered "patience" as an antidote to anger. Dante portrays "peace" as purging anger on Mount Purgatory. There is much to be said for patience. It often reflects a peaceful respite from the draining effects of anger. A person has a chance to calm down and rest, get his/her emotions back under control, and generally feel more like a reasonable human being, less dominated by only half-understood murky forces. However, patience is not always good and is often misunderstood as inactivity against wrongdoing and acceptance of a state of affairs that should not be accepted. Reinhold Neibuhr expresses the limits of patience well in his serenity prayer. "God give us the courage to change what must be changed, the patience to accept what cannot be changed, and the wisdom to know the difference." Further, are there not times when delay in itself is symptomatic of passivity and acquiescence to the most grievous injustice?

Nor is peace always good. A notable example of destructive peace is the Munich pact of 1938. Adolph Hitler had already learned that by displaying an unyielding firmness, he could bend "peace-loving" heads of European states to his will. Now Hitler demanded that Czechoslovakia cede to him the Sudeten territory on the pretext that a large part of the population was ethnic German. At Munich, Hitler met with prime ministers Neville Chamberlain of England and Edouard Daladier of France. Bullying, threatening and lying, Hitler not only convinced Chamberlain and Daladier to give him the Sudeten but made them feel good about it. Chamberlain returned home to announce to the English public that he had achieved "peace in our time."

We all know today how foolish Chamberlain was. This peace, of course, was not a true peace, but merely appeasement. Chamberlain and Daladier should not have shown patience but toughness and resolve. Months later, Hitler conquered France and nearly destroyed England as well. The "peace" lasted little more than a year, and gave Hitler a green light to pursue his attempt to conquer Europe. This kind of passivity and peace is no antidote to violence, but often leads to it. There is no question that anger can be destructive. The magnificent opening lines of Homer's *Iliad* attest to this. "Sing, goddess, the anger of Peleus' son Achilles and its devastation, which put pains one thousand fold upon the Achaians, hurled in their multitudes to the house of Hades strong souls of heroes." The bitter wrath of Achilles caused such horrifying division and destruction that there is little wonder that anger has been seen as perhaps the most dangerous of all the deadly sins. Yet, Achilles is actually quite passive in the first part of the *Iliad*, sulking in his tent because he is angry that his mistress has been taken by Agamemnon, the leader of the Greek army. His initial passivity converts into aggressive and gratuitous destructiveness.

This same pattern is described in Shakespeare's Hamlet, surely one of the towering presences of western literature. On the surface, Hamlet seems to be the antithesis of Achilles. Hamlet is given the task of killing his uncle, King Claudius, to avenge the murder of Hamlet's father. A man of intellect and refinement, Hamlet fails to carry out this violent duty, procrastinating and thinking too much as opportunities pass him by.

"Whether 'tis nobler in the mind to suffer the slings and arrows of outrageous fortune, or to take arms against a sea of troubles, and by opposing end them?" (Act III, scene1). Hamlet is on one level a noble human being, but he is too passive. By not killing the king quickly, Hamlet makes the situation far worse, allowing the king to set up the final scene in which Hamlet, Laertes, the queen and, too late, the king all meet violent deaths. By slaying the guilty Claudius earlier, Hamlet could have averted this tragic ending. Hamlet was a refined soul and a fine swordsman but his hesitation to strike when it was necessary brought all his goodness to naught and destroyed many innocent lives.

Although Hamlet is criticized as being too passive and indecisive, his behavior toward Ophelia and her father Polonius reflects a lurking anger in Hamlet. He responds harshly to Ophelia's overtures: "Get thee to a nunnery." This needlessly brutal response probably contributes to her madness and drowning. Likewise Hamlet draws his sword when he realizes someone is hiding in curtains and eavesdropping on his conversation with his mother Gertrude. He runs his sword through the figure before he knows it is Polonius. This needlessly violent action further paves the road to Ophelia's madness and death. The only figure toward whom Hamlet seems to be passive is Claudius, the murderer of his father, and the man whom he should have killed.

Achilles's anger was moved by personal pique, operating within the social code of the Homeric aristocratic hero. However, not all anger is so self-serving and without moral purpose. The Bible recounts stories where anger seems to be an appropriate response to a particular situation and the only means to meet the particular aims of virtue, peace and harmony. These stories do not idealize figures like Achilles, who are no more than machines of angry destruction. The Biblical figures can remain wholly loyal to their noble purposes and their better selves. Sometimes they must perform angry and violent deeds in defense of greater ideals, and at such times quiet and passivity are inappropriate.

Genesis 15 tells the story of five kings from Mesopotamia who invaded Canaan to put down a rebellion of four local kings. The former defeated the Canaanites and took many prisoners, including Lot, the nephew of Abraham, who had settled in the town of Sodom. Abraham knew what he had to do. This was no time to sit idle; it was a time to fight to save his nephew. Abraham collected the men of his household along with his neighboring Amorite allies, and he followed the Mesopotamian forces. Attacking them by night, Abraham caught them completely by surprise and routed them. The captives, including Lot, were rescued.

Certainly the Scriptures consider peace a great blessing, and *shalom*, the Hebrew word for peace, has entered the English language. Nevertheless, one must fight against injustice and evil, with arms when necessary. An example of the pitfalls of both excessive envy and misplaced kindness can be seen in the Biblical account of two incidents involving King Saul.

In the first incident, King Saul provokes God's rejection of his kingship of Israel because in his attack on the evil Amalekites he fails to destroy the livestock and in addition spares the life of the wicked King Agag (1 Sam. 15:7–23). Here Saul fails to discern when to be angry and when to be peaceful. He is acting indecisively, like Hamlet.

The second incident involving Saul represents a polar opposite. Here Saul orders the murder of the priests of Nob for siding with the innocent David, who is fleeing Saul's wrath. David is God's newly anointed and as such has provoked Saul's envy. Ahimelech, a priest of Nob, protests, but Saul orders his servants to kill them. When they refuse to kill the "priests of the Lord" Saul turns to the informer Doeg, the Edomite, who carries out the murderous job, killing not only the priests but also the livestock (1 Sam. 22:18–19). Eventually, God departs from Saul and will no longer answer him (1 Sam. 28:6). In this case, Saul is, like Achilles, prompted by anger motivated by jealousy.

In neither situation does Saul's response fit the precipitating event. In both cases God disapproves of his actions. In fact, the two actions can be seen as two polarities along the anger see-saw. First misplaced benignity leads Saul to spare the guilty. Then, unwarranted harshness raises its head and Saul murders the guiltless. The rabbis of the Talmud describe a voice coming from the heavens after the incident of Amalek: "Be not overly righteous." After the Nob incident there comes a voice from the heavens saying, "Be not overly wicked." One who pities the wicked will eventually be cruel when he should be merciful (Midrash Kohelet Rabbah, 7:16–17).

Three clinical cases can illustrate this point. Ralph was a man in his forties. His boss tended to criticize him publicly, and Ralph seethed internally. He began to leave work early, often stopping for a drink on the way home. He would typically come home and yell at his young son for one thing or another. When Ralph's wife attempted to intervene, he would act menacingly toward her. Ralph was obviously out of control, and like Achilles sought victims for his rage. Ralph did not respond to his boss, who really was the source of his anger. Underlying his aggression was a deep passivity.

A second clinical example illustrates Hamlet's sort of passivity. Kevin, a thirty-three-year-old man, finds it difficult to stand up to his wife. He typically goes along with her ideas even if he knows she is wrong. When Kevin and his wife come into marital therapy, he sits almost completely quiet, letting her dominate the situation. Kevin sees that she is behaving in a very rejecting way to their daughter, but he says nothing. He values peace in the house at all costs, even though his daughter is suffering from her mother's mistreatment.

A healthy alternative to both Ralph and Kevin is Ted. At work, Ted feels he has been unjustly criticized behind his back and harassed by his supervisor. He makes an appointment with his supervisor and tells him he feels angry at his behavior. One of two outcomes will occur. Either the problem will be resolved to leave Ted feeling acknowledged, or the problem will not be resolved, and Ted will know he has to move on to another position. When Ted comes home, he explains to his wife what has been happening. This allows her to understand what Ted is fighting for and not feel that he is taking his frustrations out on her. Through his active, focused and appropriate behavior, Ted is able to avoid the excessive anger of Achilles, and the passivity of Hamlet as well.

Zealous vengeance is an act that modern man finds very disturbing and uncivilized. So does Scripture, enjoining its readers, "Thou shalt not take revenge." God rebuked Elijah, the great prophet, for being overly zealous. God is also described as being gracious and merciful, and slow to anger (Joel 2:13). However, this should not be interpreted as God's acquiescence to injustice. Sometimes, only action can bring about the higher aims of virtuous peace and harmony.

Indeed, there are many times when God Himself is described as becoming angry (e.g., Exod. 4:14; Num. 11:1, 10; 12:9; 22:22; 25:3–4; 32:10, 13, 14; Deut. 7:4, 29:20, 23, 27) and action becomes the only effective means to handle a serious problem. However, God's anger is not to be confused with a cold calculated revenge. The idea that "revenge is a dish best served cold" is quite foreign to Biblical thought. God's anger towards his people is hot, not cold, and motivated by His love for them. An expression often used to describe God's anger is "His nostrils burned" (e.g., Exod. 4:14, Num. 11:10), and indeed this expression is used to express anger generally (Gen. 4:5, Exod. 32:19). His interaction with the world is not detached as is Zeus's, looking down on humanity from Mount Olympus. Biblical figures should not go through life like Achilles as machines of angry destruction. However, neither should they, like Hamlet, be paralyzed with inactivity. They must remain wholly loyal to their nobler purposes and their better selves.

Consider the Biblical story of Phinehas and his confrontation with immorality. The Israelites were encamped at Shittim. The Moabites had failed to destroy them with Balaam's curses and now sent their daughters to seduce Israelite men and lead them into the idolatrous and degrading rites of their deity, Baal-Peor. The plan seemed to be working. Many Israelite men were entrapped, and God sent a plague to punish them. Moses set up special courts to deal with the crisis, but with little apparent effect; the orgies went on and so did the plague. Then Zimri ben Salu, a prince of the tribe of Simeon, brought a Midianite woman through the Israelite camp, flaunting her in full view of Moses and his advisors. The two proceeded to Zimri's tent. Moses and the judges wept, perhaps from sheer frustration, but they seemed unable to stop Zimri. National disaster threatened. Then Phinehas arose. There is no record that prior to this moment he had ever done anything noteworthy or had ever held any public position. Now, however, he saw that the plague was spreading, and that the leaders could not act. He was morally repulsed and could not remain inactive. He took upon himself the great responsibility that that moment required, working completely on his own with no authorization from the leaders, but in consonance with law. Although not an experienced warrior, he took a spear in his hand. At great personal risk, he followed Zimri and the Midianite woman into the tent where, finding them in *flagrante delicto*, he thrust the spear through them both, transfixing them in a way that showed exactly what they were doing (Num. 25:7). "And he came after the Israelite man into the tent, and he speared both the Israelite man and the woman through her belly." The result of Phinehas's zealous and unselfish act was that the plague finally ceased after having killed twenty-four thousand people. Phinehas was compelled by a belief in righteousness, in the need to honor God's name, to save lives and to prevent a potential moral breakdown of the entire nation. It is important to stress that he was not driven by a thirst for blood or attention, and this distinguishes his actions from those of Achilles. God confirmed Phinehas's act by establishing two covenants with him: (1) His "treaty of peace" (Num. 25:12) and (2) a treaty of "everlasting priesthood" (Num. 25:13). Phinehas now joined the rest of the family of Aaron as a full-fledged priest, serving in the Tabernacle, a privilege he had not held before. This was the suitable reward for one who had brought about atonement for the Israelites, which is one of the priest's main responsibilities. By acting as decisively as he did, Phinehas saved many lives and quieted God's anger at His people. This was so unlike Hamlet, whose indecision brought about the death of a number of people, including himself. Phinehas, by doing what the law required of him although violence was not his usual way, struck the blow that stopped the plague and ultimately saved many lives and perhaps the essential character of a great Biblical religion.

Modern sensibilities recoil from a story of vengeance. Yet, this is an important story. What is of essence here is that Phinehas reacted and that Hamlet did not. It is sometimes right and healthy to become angry. Not to become angry in the face of great wrong or danger can breed an insidious passivity that will cast a blind eye at all sorts of wrongs. Moreover, such inaction tends to diminish one's sense of self. It is an evasion of responsibility.

The story of Phinehas must not be interpreted as glorifying violence or macho per se, but there are times when action is necessary, and in such a case, zeal and conviction need not be a mindless fanaticism but instead can represent the deepest spiritual love of God, of goodness and of right. Achilles and Hamlet are two sides of the see-saw. Achilles is a paradigm of anger and Hamlet of indecision disguised as peace. Phinehas rejects both extremes, demonstrating a righteous anger in the service of an overriding moral cause. People will grow if they develop the strength and stamina to take action when it must be taken. Often, like Phinehas, we may find ourselves acting alone—but so be it. The alternatives can be the self-absorbed vengeance of an Achilles or the endless inaction and self-recriminations of a Hamlet.

Yet anger is not always good. Moses was a deeply humble and compassionate man, who had learned much of the meaning of peace and of goodness both from God's direct teaching and from his own life experience. Yet, he was not at times free of strong or even violent reactions. Let us view four incidents in his life. In two, his strong reaction was appropriate, but in the other two it was not. (See Schwartz and Kaplan, 2004, p. 99–101).

Moses was raised as a prince in Pharaoh's palace, but the princess, his step-mother, had informed him of his Hebrew origin. When he grew old enough, Moses went forth to see the Hebrews oppressed in their slavery, and his heart went out to them. A certain Egyptian overseer was beating a slave. Looking around and seeing no other Egyptians, Moses killed the man and hid his body in the sand. Moses had been careless. He could accomplish nothing for the slaves by killing one taskmaster. Perhaps the taskmaster did not even deserve to be killed for beating the slave. More dangerous for Moses was that he had been careless of his own safety. Someone, perhaps one of the slaves, reported Moses' deed to Pharaoh, who sought to arrest Moses and to execute him. Moses was forced to flee Egypt. He returned only many years later when God sent him to lead the Hebrew exodus from Egypt. Again, Moses' killing of the Egyptian was noble, fed by his compassion for the slaves. However, it was ill considered in that it was perhaps too violent and, in fact, accomplished little, while putting Moses himself in danger (Exod. 2:11–15).

Moses had endured many months of dealing with Pharaoh's cruelties toward the Hebrews and with his constant reneging on promises to let them depart from Egypt. After the ninth plague—darkness—Pharaoh told Moses that "you will never see my face again for on the day you will see my face you shall surely die" (Exod. 10:28). Moses could deal with the frustrations and disappointments of his labors and even with the hardships and sufferings of his people, but until now there had always seemed some small hope that Pharaoh could still be dealt with peaceably and success-fully. But now Pharaoh himself seemed to be rejecting with finality all of Moses' goodwill as well as his own human duty to the Hebrews. It seems to have pained Moses deeply to see a human being so persistent in his foolish wrongdoing and purposefully hurtling to his own self-destruction. And Moses indeed became angry: "And Moses departed in anger from before Pharaoh" (Exod. 11:8). There is no indication in the Scripture that Moses' anger was in any way wrong or unjust.

Many years passed. By now, Moses had long been the leader of the Israelites in the wilderness. The people came with a legitimate request for water. God told Moses to speak to a certain rock and it would bring forth water. However, feeling that the people's request was out of line and rebellious, Moses overreacted, addressing them harshly, "Hear ye rebels" (Num. 20:10). In his anger, Moses then smote the rock with his staff instead of speaking to it as he was commanded. God punished him by decreeing that he would not be permitted to enter the Land of Israel.

Moses came down from Mt. Sinai after forty days of study with God Himself. He was bringing to the Israelite people the Ten Commandments inscribed by God on two tablets of stone. Moses walked down the mountain and saw people worshipping the golden calf. "And he saw the calf and the dancing, and Moses reacted angrily and cast the tablets from his hand, breaking them at the base of the mountain" (Exod. 32:19). Moses' anger was in this case very suitable. The people had behaved badly, and they did not at that moment deserve the divinely made tablets. God later signaled approval of Moses' act by spending a second forty days with him on the mountain and by giving him a second set of tablets.

A vivid example of undirected and gratuitous anger is the behavior of the former Chicago Cub superstar, Sammy Sosa. A player credited with helping to restore interest in baseball in the late 1990s, Sosa's hitting had declined steadily over several years. He came under increasing criticism from fans in 2004, and at the end of a very frustrating season received a lukewarm endorsement from Dusty Baker, his manager. After a devastating team collapse during the last week of the year, Baker said he would welcome Sosa back in 2005, but only if he prepared himself physically and mentally. Sosa responded by sitting out the last game of the year, claiming he was sick. To make matters worse, Sosa came late for the game, did not dress, and left the game during the first inning. Further, he lied as to when he left, claiming he did not leave till the seventh inning, though a security camera showed that he had indeed left during the first inning.

Sosa's behavior stemmed from hurt and anger at his manager. He felt unjustly singled out for criticism and blame for his team's demise. But, like Achilles, he was initially passive. And then, like Achilles again, Sosa exploded in an inappropriate way that was both self-destructive and insulting to his teammates who had generally supported him. Ultimately, he was traded to the Baltimore Orioles.

Sosa's behavior vacillated between passivity and anger. How much healthier it would have been for him to have been able to sit down and talk with his manager privately and tell him he felt wronged. He could have done this in an honest and constructive way. It is important to stress that a person can be righteous without behaving aggressively. One can disagree without being disagreeable. Consider the Biblical story of Noah.

Noah lived in a time of terrible social breakdown. People acted toward each other with almost unrestrained violence, respecting neither persons nor property. Yet Noah himself was a hardworking, mild-mannered man who found grace in the eyes of God. In fact, the Hebrew name "*Noach*" with the letters scrambled ("*chen*") means "grace" or "pleasantness." He was not a politician, not persuasive, not a great orator, not argumentative. Yet in a world which had become viciously competitive, Noah could maintain his own goodness. When God sent the flood, it was a man like Noah who had the character to spend years building the ark, and then take care of a multitude of animals, each with its own unique needs.

Yet, although not combative by nature, Noah used his abilities to maintain his integrity and to do what had to be done. He did not go along with the crowd, nor did he try to appease them. He disagreed with those around him but he was not disagreeable. He was not a hero in the Greek sense, and perhaps not even a risk taker, but he was a righteous man. He did not compromise or derogate his mission of saving humanity and animals and rebuilding human history. He did not appease or give in to the evils of his society, but he remained an essentially pleasant man.

We conclude this chapter with an incident illustrating the oscillation between anger and passivity, and how important it is to get off this seesaw to achieve a righteous response to a provocative situation. For a number of years, a university department rented parking spaces from an adjoining lot owned by a church. Individual faculty members rented individual spaces from the collective. Over the years a pervasive and annoying problem developed. Students and others parked at will in reserved spots, with almost complete impunity. University police would give a ticket if the owner of the spot contacted them. However, the intruders rarely paid and the lack of payment did not result in any penalty.

Faculty and staff in the departmental parking collective seemed paralyzed, unwilling to take any steps to counter the situation. The passivity of the members of the parking collective left them totally unable to assert ownership of their spaces. Finally, the collective acted, but in a very exaggerated way. It hired a towing company to tow away illegal parkers. This in itself was good, but the way in which it was handled reflected an exaggerated anger. To begin with, the towing company was focused on towing as many cars as it could, whether or not they belonged in the lot. Indeed, during the first week of operation, they towed away the cars of several legitimate parking space owners, even with the parking tags clearly visible. Second, the fee demanded to release a car was almost triple the amount agreed on with the parking collective. In addition, complaints by affected members were summarily dismissed by the collective. Finally, members of the collective were actually instructed not to warn people whom they saw parking illegally in the lot. The rationale was that the towing company was paid only by the cars that they towed, so warning people was defeating their purpose.

These instructions totally confused the relationship of the departmental parking collective to the towing company. The aim of the department was to have clear parking spots. The aim of the towing company was to maximize the number of cars towed. Yet the department in effect had abdicated its ownership of the parking spaces to the towing company. It had seesawed from a passivity to an excessive reaction of anger, which ironically still left it passive.

What would be a healthy Biblical reaction to this situation? Simply, use a towing company but strongly insist on accountability from them. Insist on careful criteria before a car may be towed. It seems reasonable to present the towing company with a list of the license plates of the legitimate cars, with the presence of either an acceptable license plate or a tag serving as a defense against being towed. Without either an acceptable license or a tag, cars should be considered fair game to be towed. At the same time, there is need to warn illegal parkers. The aim is clear—to have a clear parking lot, not to create business for the towing company. Finally, the towing company should be compelled to be responsive to any false tows and to compensate the injured party. This is what a righteous response would entail, and it would avoid the see-saw between anger and appeasement disguised as peace.

Chapter Four

Love: An Escape from the Lust-Chastity See-Saw

"And the Lord God said, It is not good that man should be alone. I will make him a helpmeet opposite."

—Genesis 2:18

The fourth deadly sin is lust. Lust denotes an unrestrained expression of sexual impulse and is implicated in many immoral and illegal behaviors. Yet, the physical sexual desire beneath lust is perfectly natural. What is improper or destructive is the reduction of the other or indeed oneself into an object of lust and the disconnection of the material from the spiritual. Prudentius has suggested chastity as an antidote to lust. To the extent that chastity denotes modesty, it is clearly preferable to unbridled lust. The problem lies in the way it has sometimes been interpreted. Chastity may imply not simply modesty or purity but a repudiation of the physical aspect of a relationship. It can be devastating to the relationship between husband and wife, or parent and child. This view of chastity is hardly preferable to lust.

The Biblical virtue of love represents a healthy alternative to both lust and chastity, one which unites body and soul and allows for a healthy relationship between people. To begin with, God is portrayed as creating man in his own image as an act of love, and giving him dominion over the world (Gen. 1:27–28). Love at its best is the yearning of one's soul for goodness and for the Creator.

Love in modern times has often been equated with unbridled sexuality on the one hand and an unrooted, spacey universalism on the other. In the best sense love is an action in an ongoing relationship, where the physical reflects the spiritual. There is a world of difference between "loving" someone and simply "making love" on the one hand, and "being in love" on the other.

Andy was a handsome strapping young fellow in his late twenties. Women fought over him and thought of him as a "great lover." But Andy's behavior consisted of a series of short chaotic relationships, which tended to remain quite shallow and peter out fairly quickly. Women would leave a relationship with him with the feeling that they had never really gotten to know him. Nor did Andy show any interest in getting to know them as people. He was a "lover" but he could not love. Theresa, in contrast, was always involved in one cause or another and claimed to love all humanity. Yet she seemed totally uninvolved in taking care of her own husband and children. Nor did she see much of her parents. In what sense could Theresa be said to love?

Love at its best is the yearning of one's soul for goodness and for the Creator. We use the term love today in a loose way to describe what are in fact different sorts of experiences. We may love a new pair of shoes, but this is likely to be simply the satisfying of basic needs or superficial desires. One may be strongly attracted to a person and feel he/she is in love; yet this may be nothing more than infatuation. On what is the highest sort of love between people based? There can be a friendship in which people help each other to grow and to create, in which each calls forth from the other a higher reaching for goodness. In such a friendship, the people support each other in reaching toward God and goodness whether in great ideas or small behaviors. Kindness and a sense of the presence of God are the essence of this highest level of love. Yet much in our culture belies this interpretation. In fact, much of the view of love in contemporary culture seems to derive from classical Greek rather than Biblical sources.

Let us view two types of relationships: 1) men-women, and 2) parents-children.

MEN AND WOMEN

In Euripides's tragedy *Hippolytus*, Hippolytus displays a chastity toward his stepmother Phaedra that does not simply reflect loyalty to his father

Theseus but is also contaminated with a pervasive and unrelenting misogyny: "I can never satisfy my hate for women, no! not even though some say this is ever my theme, for of a truth they always are evil. So either let some one prove them chaste, or let me still trample on them for ever" (l. 664–667). The only good woman is the chaste woman, which in practice becomes the asexual woman.

This view is illustrated in a Greek myth that has been reproduced in modern versions as George Bernard Shaw's *Pygmalion*, and as Lerner and Loewe's *My Fair Lady*. Pygmalion was unable to find any woman that he could love. All were imperfect. Finally, Pygmalion built a statue that embodied the symmetric perfection of womanhood. Enraptured with his own work, Pygmalion embraced the cold statue, and the gods rewarded him by magically turning the statue into a live woman, Galatea.

In contrast, the Biblical God has specifically commanded people to "be fruitful and multiply" (Gen. 1:28). God creates woman as a companion for man because it is not good for man to be alone (Gen. 2:18). The importance of the physical aspect of a love relationship between man and woman is clearly stated in Genesis 4:1: "And man knew Eve his wife, and she conceived." Love integrates the physical and the emotional, avoiding the pitfalls of a soulless lust, or a totally idealized withdrawal from physical contact.

The physical aspect of a marital relationship is not to be rejected, nor woman denigrated. However, it must be part of love rather than serving an immoral aim. Consider Joseph's rejection of the overtures of Potiphar's wife in the Hebrew Scriptures. Joseph's rejection is not based on any sense of misogyny or denial of sexuality (as is that of Hippolytus), but rather on a sense that he would be sinning against God if he were to betray both God and his master: "Behold, my master, having me, knoweth not what is in the house, and he hath put all that he hath in my hand; . . . but thee, because thou art his wife. How then can I do this great wickedness, and sin against God?" (Gen. 39: 8–9). It is not sexuality that is evil, or woman, but the fact that the wife of Potiphar is attempting to lure Joseph into adulterous betrayal of his master.

Unfortunately, however, much of Greek and western literature does see the sexual woman as inherently evil. One of the saddest themes emerging in Victorian society is the split between whore and madonna. Wives and ladies were supposed to be chaste in the sense of being asexual, not simply to be modest, while men could enjoy sex with barmaids and wenches. The real woman is feared, and the ideal woman is elevated.

The husband's repugnance toward and rejection of the physical needs of his wife and the female dissatisfaction with such imposed chastity has been a subject of Freud and Kinsey and is illustrated in Jonathan Swift's satire of the travels of Gulliver. One of the kingdoms Gulliver visits is that of *La Puta*, which is ruled by a philosopher king in the Platonic mold (Swift here is intentionally building on Martin Luther's term "the whore [*la puta*] reason"). Starved by the lack of concrete attention paid her by her abstract and distant husband, the wife of the philosopher king has left him and is now living in the lower city with a coachman, who beats her when he is drunk, but at least acknowledges her existence.

Why is there such a fear of a real woman in Greek and contemporary western society? Let us look at what Greek mythology says about the earliest appearance of woman. This is the story of Pandora, a name that means all gifted. Zeus, the father of the gods, decides to make life difficult for the first men by withholding from them the knowledge of fire. However, Prometheus, a titan and an uncle of Zeus, has his own ideas.

Prometheus steals fire from Mt Olympus, the home of the gods, and hiding it in a hollow fennel stalk, brings it to man, enabling him to become more autonomous and to survive. Zeus soon learns what has been done and, enraged, he plots great harm against man. He calls on the various gods and demigods and has each of them contribute to the making of a new creature. One gives her a beautiful form and appearance. Another gives her grace, and others give her wonderful skills like weaving. However, the sly god Hermes gives her terrible morals—the "morals of a bitch."

Zeus sends Pandora to Epimetheus, the naive brother of the wise Prometheus. Impressed with Pandora's beauty, Epimetheus ignores or forgets his brother's warning never to accept any gift from Zeus. One day, Pandora's curiosity gets the better of her and she decides to open the box that Zeus sent along with her. The box contains all the evils in the world, which fly out as soon as Pandora opens it. All the evils in the world today are there because this first woman released them. But perhaps worse, she manages to hold hope in the box, so that it is hope alone that is unavailable to people. Hope is still locked in the box. In this myth, woman is the villain and Zeus gives her to man not as a precious gift but as an act of revenge. Pandora is sly, dishonest and secretive, and her immature inability to control her curiosity brings endless anguish on mankind. She is described as "a race apart."

The negative view of woman and of love is clear. Pandora has been created and sent by Zeus to punish man because Prometheus has stolen fire for man, making him more autonomous. Woman is sent to strip him of his newly won autonomy and make him subservient once again. Woman and love are seen as a trap for man, designed to keep him enslaved. Only a fool like Epimetheus would be deceived by her beauty.

This view has been articulated in the lyrics of Frank Sinatra's popular song "The Tender Trap" from the movie of the same name. In this song, Sinatra speaks of how a woman's "laughing eyes" and "sighing sighs" lull a man along until unwittingly he falls into a trap. This trap is compounded when the woman kisses and embraces the man, making him feel terrible about being alone. Suddenly the man realizes he has fallen in love and there is no way of escaping it. Thus, woman has led man into a tender trap.

Although this song is good-natured, philosophical and accepting, the view of a relationship with a woman as a trap has far more sinister and disturbing roots. There is no more striking theme in ancient mythology than that of the "vagina dentata." As its name implies, vagina dentata literally is a portrayal of the female vagina with teeth, like a shark. Woman then is seen as the castrator of man and a sexual relationship as a not-so-tender trap and is, in fact, his undoing. Indeed, Hesiod portrays the unborn Chronus reaching from the womb of his mother and castrating his understandably surprised father Ouranos.

And indeed, Greek literature portrays woman at best as a necessary evil. In Euripides's tragedy *Medea,* the protagonist Jason laments that "it would be better for children to have come into this world by some other means, and women never to have existed. Then life would be good." Medea, strikingly, shares this debased view of women, saying "it would be better to serve in battle three times than have one child" (l. 250–52, 573–75).

The classical Greek fear of a real woman (and sexuality) has pervaded the Hollywood image of love. In its attack on chastity, Hollywood has oscillated to the other extreme of lust, with scantily clad or even seminaked women selling everything from beer to professional football. The sexual act has been separated from love and converted into simple recreational activity, devoid of emotional content. Sexual relations have been converted into mechanical acts. One "screws" or "bangs" rather than makes love. The bedroom is turned into a hardware store and the bed into a workbench. The act of lovemaking has been converted into a purely mechanical act of lust.

This stratagem may temporarily alleviate man's dilemma, allowing him to fulfill his sexual needs while avoiding emotional attachment. By draining the sexual act of its emotional tone, man converts woman into a sexual object with no ability to entrap him. But this resolution can hardly be satisfactory in the long run. Such relations with women are distant and devoid of the intimacy that real love requires. The physical act of sex becomes disconnected from spiritual intimacy.

Much of human thought counsels, either implicitly or explicitly, against loving too much for fear of excessive attachment. Loving too much is seen as engendering dependency or possessiveness, where it is feared that the lover cannot give the love object any freedom or respect his/her individuality. And this is perhaps the problem, that the love object is seen as an object and not experienced as a separate being. Perhaps as a result of this, we have come to fear deep love and have come to use the term so loosely as to lose its original meaning.

An interesting aspect of the Pandora story is that although she is portrayed as a "race apart," and the source of man's downfall, she is never described as much of a personality. She is simply a plaything of Zeus sent to the world for the specific purpose of bearing trouble. There is no personality development, and when she removes the lid of the jar, it is all from curiosity, more foolish than malicious, although she does not seem to lack malice.

Pandora is portrayed very differently from Eve, in the Genesis account of creation. Eve is not described as a race apart as is Pandora, but in one creation account as being created along with man in God's image (Gen. 1:27) and in the second as taken from one of Adam's ribs (Gen. 2:22). Moreover, she is described by man as "bone of my bones, and flesh of my flesh" (Gen. 2:23). Clearly, man and woman are from the same planet! She is a helpmeet for Adam and not a punishment, but the Hebrew words denoting helpmeet are very significant. Woman is described as an *ezer kenegdo*, literally meaning helpmeet opposite him (Gen. 2:18). Love between man and woman is then the creative tension of two independent forces.

The Bible does not see the human being as a piece of sugar, who will melt if one loves or is loved. The Bible expresses this human need for love in the form of a commandment: "And you shall love the Lord your God with all your heart and with all your soul and with all your might." The beautiful words between lovers in the Song of Songs describe a deeply sensual and reciprocal love relationship between a man and woman that is clearly an alternative to both lust and chastity. For example,

> I am my beloved's
> And his desire is toward me,
> Come, my beloved, let us go forth into the field;
> Let us lodge in the villages,
> Let us get up early to the vineyards;
> Let us see whether the vine hath budded,
> Whether the vine-blossom be opened,
> And the pomegranates be in flower;
> There will I give thee my love. (7:11–13)

It should be stressed that many Biblical commentators interpret this passage metaphorically as a description of the love between God and His people. And this is important. God is not to be conceived as an unmoved mover, but as a lover. The Bible begins with a supreme act of love— God's creation of the world. In the Biblical account, God created the world and humankind in an act of love, and God is not squeamish about showing His love. When a person truly recognizes the greatness of God's creation and the depth of His love and kindness, one cannot help but be moved to love the Creator who gave him/her all these wonders as an act of pure love. Once again it should be stressed that the Hebrew Bible does not see the human being as a piece of sugar, who will melt if he loves too much. The Bible expresses this human need to love in the form of a commandment: "And you shall love the lord your God with all your heart and with all your soul and with all your might."

The Hebrew Bible sees the relationship between body and soul and between man and woman as integrated rather than disconnected. Hebrew thought sees no opposition between body and soul, or between flesh and spirit. The human body and soul are both sacred, both created by God. They can and must function in harmony to fulfill God's purposes in the world. Emotion, intellect and body are all integral components of a human being and there is no opposition between body and soul or flesh and spirit.

The creation of people in Genesis is the beautiful culmination of six days of creation by a benevolent and all-wise God. All the world has been prepared and made ready for them. Finally, late on the sixth day, God is ready. "Let us make man." He gathered dust from the earth to make the body and then breathed into him the breath of life. God's first words to the human race constitute an instruction, a command and a blessing all together. "Be fruitful and multiply and fill the earth." The people are not created by God to lighten His workload or to be His messenger in a nasty trick. Chapter II in Genesis tells how God taught Adam all about the plants and animals, and Adam with his new knowledge of science learned from the divine scientist classified and gave names to them all. The form of the blessing is significant, for what God gives people is something very special to Him. It is the gift of creativity and of independence of thought and action which includes even the power to act against God's wishes. No parent ever gave an adolescent child the keys to his car with less reluctance.

The creation of woman is part of God's emphasis on the importance of a relationship. With all Adam's achievements, he was unfulfilled. God saw that it was not good for a man to be lonely. And He put Adam into a deep sleep and separated part of his body, thus dividing the original human into two beings, a man and a woman. Eve is created as a helpmeet opposite to man, rather than as a curse like Pandora.

As we have emphasized previously, Biblical people were never designed to be mere automatons, puppets of God like the first people in so many of the myths. However, Eve, prompted by the evil snake, did not see it this way. She seems to have believed the serpent for a moment and to have seen the God of the Bible as if He were Zeus. She was misled into seeing God's prohibition to Adam as an attempt to enslave him rather than to ensure that he used his autonomy to carry out his role in God's creation of the world. As a loyal helpmeet, Eve stood by Adam and tried to help him free himself from what he had been misled into believing was his subjugation.

Eve was mistaken in her judgment, as any of us can be, but she was acting honestly in what she believed would foster Adam's best interests. Eve's aim was not to hinder man but to help him. And Adam had nothing to fear from her, or from her sexuality. Biblical commentary on this passage emphasizes that Adam must not blame Eve for causing him to eat of the forbidden fruit.

What exactly are the consequences? Adam and Eve disobey God and they are expelled from Eden after this act of disobedience. They will ultimately face death. They will have to struggle and to work in the sweat of their brow. But are these things necessarily so bad in themselves or do these very acts give life its meaning?

Even after having done wrong, Eve did not wholly lose her cool. When confronted by God, she explained what happened in dignified, almost poetic, language. "The serpent beguiled me." (Beguile is not the sort of word one often sees in freshman English papers.) God still loved Eve, and his words to her are certainly not a curse and not even so much a punishment as an attempt to help her define her situation.

There would now be pain for her in the bearing and raising of children, "and to your husband shall be your desire and he shall rule over you." This phrase was never intended to give the man license to lord it over an inferior slave/partner. Remember, she had been created as a helpmeet opposite him (an *ezer kenegdo*). What it does mean is that the woman seems to have some conflict over her drive to freedom. She wants to be independent of the husband, but at the same time does not want to. This is a problem of which she must be aware. In the eyes of God she remains a person free and indeed obligated to be moral and to develop her full human abilities and creativity and to learn to make right choices and decisions in her life. She, like the man, will find her fullest freedom and creativity through her service to God.

Although the two people were sent out of the Garden, their humanity and greatness remained intact. They could still have wonderful lives. God Himself signaled His recognition and empathy in their new situation by giving them garments to cover the nakedness that had so worried them.

Although woman is told she will bear children in pain, it is also true that she is given the name Eve (*Chava* in Hebrew), meaning mother of life, only upon her expulsion from Eden. Adam and Eve are now aware of their nakedness, but does not God clothe them in animal skins? And does

He not provide for the continuation of human life through Seth, the third son of Adam and Eve, even after Cain murdered Abel?

Certainly, the Biblical message in all this is far different from that portrayed in the Greek world. In the Biblical view, attachment is not seen as inconsistent with freedom, nor woman as a block to man's autonomy. Nor are sexual relations with a woman a fearsome trap for man. In the Biblical view there is no stigma attached to woman, nor is sexual love to be avoided and deemed contradictory to spiritual love. When Genesis refers to Adam "knowing" Eve, it clearly refers to both a physical and a spiritual knowing. Love integrates the physical and the emotional, avoiding the pitfalls of a soulless lust, or a totally idealized withdrawal from physical contact.

The Biblical view is clear that the highest state of existence for any person is marriage. All through the Book of Genesis, women of remarkable intelligence and character are great personalities in their own right, contributing much to the story of God and humanity, and at the same time are wonderfully important figures within their families, supporting their husbands when the situation warrants and opposing their husbands when that seems the right course.

A physical relationship with a woman is not to be feared as woman is not seen as a devouring earth mother or castrator but as a nurturer. This is the difference between the way the great fish is described in the Biblical story of Jonah, as a belly or womb that saves man's life, as opposed to the way the white whale is described in *Moby Dick,* where the fish's teeth literally have sawn off Ahab's leg.

Nothing can illustrate this difference more sharply that an analysis of the Greek and Hebrew terms for womb or uterus. The Greek term is *hystera,* from which terms like hysteria and hysterectomy emerge. The *hystera* is a source of labile and even mercurial affect and woman, even in the Freudian scheme, is seen as unstable and an unreliable source of morality. She is to be feared, as she is not a source of love and compassion but of unstable, hysterical emotions.

The Biblical term for womb is *rehem*, which has a quite different connotation. It is related to the Hebrew word *rahamim,* meaning mercy or compassion, the highest compliment to bestow on someone, and a term used to describe God Himself—as one who creates life and has compassion for his children. Woman is anything but unstable in this view. Instead she provides a secure base for human development. This "secure parenting" is a major issue in contemporary psychology. Children need a secure foundation on which to grow.

Biblical women are typically morally strong figures who express great humanity to people and in service to God. Women like Sarah and Rebecca play highly important roles in carrying out the mission that God has given them of building a new faith and nation based on monotheism, wisdom and love. To carry out this mission, woman may need to do many things, beginning with the support she gives as wife and mother and going on to a wide range of emotional, economic and social activities. This is the "woman of valor" as described in Proverbs 31.

Woman was a great blessing to man, his equal and opposite, and his best supporter, who could meet him on his own ground and share life with him as an equal and an important being in her own right. Eve is a wonderful prototype and role model for all later women. Even after the people ate from the forbidden fruit and had been sent away from the beautiful Garden of Eden, Adam signals his appreciation for this woman by giving her a new name, Eve, mother of all life. Mark Twain, in his story *Adam's Diary*, has Adam write that he treasured Eve more and more as time went on, for he learned that although they had been sent out of the Garden, wherever she was, there for him was Eden. This is obviously an expression of the Biblical virtue of love, not of lust or chastity.

PARENTS AND CHILDREN

The Biblical virtue of love is expressed also in the relationship between parents and children. Love of children should not mean that one cannot correct them. For parents must teach them. The deadly sin of lust here is often expressed as possessiveness where the child is seen as an object. In the Greek tragedy of *Medea*, Euripides portrays Medea as killing her two young sons in order to hurt their father Jason. The converse is parental abandonment, physical withdrawal or indifference, which reflects the antidote of chastity or abstinence. The goddess Artemis's withdrawal from the dying Hippolytus is an example of such behavior—she presumably cannot stand to see his suffering so she abandons him (Euripides, *Hippolytus*, lines 1432–1433). Another example of withdrawal is Hagar's treatment of Ishmael in the desert. After the bread and water given to them by Abraham are gone, she casts the child under a shrub and goes some distance off, saying, "Let me not look upon the death of the child" (Gen. 21:16).

Neither reflects the healthy parental love exemplified in the Hebrew Bible. This love is illustrated in the story of Hannah and her son Samuel. Hannah goes to the Tabernacle to pray for a child. Within a year, she gives birth to Samuel, and in gratitude consecrates him to service to God in the Tabernacle, even though she is losing the pleasure of having him at home. Hannah gives physical expression to her love for Samuel by making him a special robe to wear in the Tabernacle and bringing him new ones as he grows. Hannah neither possesses Samuel as an object, nor does she abandon him.

Yet the physical is not all there is to parental love. If a child grows up with physical gifts that substitute for love, the child may feel unloved when he grows up. Jacqueline Kennedy Onassis was quoted in her last years as saying that if you bungle your children, nothing else makes any difference. While children can certainly benefit from an occasional treat, it is far more important for them to learn a measure of self-control when it comes to their own perceived needs. The Bible teaches that it is important for children to be loved in ways that foster the virtues of kindness, honesty, hard work, diligence and the like. It is far less important for them to own a particular toy or game or item of clothing.

There is ample room for misunderstanding around even simple encounters between parents and children. Consider the reaction of traditionally religious parents to the announcement of their teenage daughter that she does not believe in God and will no longer attend worship services. It is difficult for the parents to perceive this action as anything other than a slap in the face to them and an estrangement from the basic values of the family. How can they respond? If the parents insist that the daughter continue to attend services, she may go reluctantly and may feel resentful that the parents did not respect her desires.

Consider the parents' alternative of disconnecting from their daughter and letting her go her own way. This may prove equally disastrous. The daughter may unconsciously feel abandoned and reject all moral and religious teaching and become involved in unhealthy relationships or even addictions. Here parents can be faulted for not providing helpful guidance. The Biblical principle is clear here: "You shall teach your children diligently" (Deut. 6:7).

What should parents do? There is no simple answer, given the often problematic nature of the parent-child relationship. What is generally important is that parents teach their values and wisdom in a way so that the child feels respected and accepted. This is one of the great challenges of parenting, and methods that work for one generation may not work for the next.

The underlying question is this. Does the child see the parents as encouraging his development and independence (i.e., as a source of love) or does he see them as blocking him and trying to keep him dependent (i.e., as a source of possessiveness)? Alternatively, does he see his parents as ignoring him completely (i.e., as a source of abandonment)? Analogously, does the parent encourage the child to grow as far as he can, even if this means surpassing the parent? Or does the parent try to undercut the child, either through possessiveness or withdrawal, and thus maintain control over him or her?

The haunting Mexican movie *Like Water for Chocolate* illustrates this theme vividly. Tita is the last of three daughters born to a respected, affluent family, and inherits a dubious birthright. According to Mexican tradition as portrayed in this movie, the youngest daughter is forbidden to marry so she can care for her aging widowed mother. Tita is groomed for this position by becoming the cook for the family. As Tita blossoms into a beautiful young woman, she falls in love with the handsome Pedro. Tita's mother, Elena, however, refuses to allow Pedro and Tita to marry, but instead offers Pedro the hand of her eldest daughter Rosaura. To add insult to injury, Elena commissions Tita to prepare the wedding feast.

Consider in contrast the Biblical story of Naomi and Ruth. Naomi, her husband, and their two sons leave Judah to reside in Moab. Here, Naomi's husband dies and her two sons marry women of Moab, Orpah and Ruth. When Naomi's two sons also die, she sets out to return to Judah accompanied by her two daughters-in-law. Naomi blesses her daughters-in-law and tells them to go back to Moab, to their own people. They both cry and insist that they will return with their mother-in-law to Judah. Naomi again urges them to go back to their families, stating that she is too old to have more sons for them to marry (Ruth 1:11–12). Naomi does not try to bind her daughters-in-law to her but unselfishly urges them to go on their way to find husbands. This in itself is remarkable. Naomi seems to overcome her bitterness and what must have been her isolation as a widow to recognize the need of these two women to have their own lives, even if it means Naomi herself will be abandoned in the process. She is a strong and healthy enough woman to realize that her daughters-in-law are not simply objects to serve her.

Orpah kisses her mother-in-law and departs, but Ruth will have none of it. In a moving speech, Ruth expresses her devotion to Naomi as a person in her own right rather than as only a producer of a son. Ruth refuses to abandon Naomi. Indeed she bonds to Naomi's land, people, and God.

And Ruth says, "Entreat me not to leave thee, or to return from following after thee: for whither thou goest, I will go; and where thou lodgest, I will lodge: thy people shall be my people, and thy God my God. Where thou diest, will I die and there will I be buried: the Lord do so to me, and more also, if ought but death part thee and me" (Ruth 1:16–17).

Naomi is not afraid to let Ruth grow. Ruth is not driven to abandon Naomi, and Naomi accepts Ruth among her people. This beautiful reciprocity continues throughout the story. Naomi continuously encourages and helps Ruth to fulfill her own needs, and Ruth is certain to include Naomi in any good fortune she may experience. Ruth meets Boaz, a kinsman of Naomi's late husband, who is greatly moved by Ruth's treatment of Naomi: "It hath fully been told me, all that thou hadst done unto thy mother-in-law since the death of thy husband." (2:11) Naomi continues to look out for Ruth's welfare unselfishly. Rather than diminish Ruth's self-esteem or block her development, Naomi instructs Ruth in what she should do to win Boaz (3:1–4).

Ruth follows Naomi's advice, and ultimately marries Boaz. She does not fail to include Naomi in her happiness. Naomi becomes the nurse to their son and is even described by the neighbors as the child's mother: "And he shall be unto thee a restorer of life and a nourisher of thine old age; for thy daughter-in-law, who loveth thee, who is better to thee than seven sons, hath borne him. And Naomi took the child, and laid it in her bosom, and became nurse unto it. And the women her neighbors gave it a name, saying, 'There is a son born to Naomi.' And they called his name Obed; he is the father of Jesse, the father of David" (4:5–17). The Moabite Ruth is a fit ancestress of the Davidic dynasty.

What are the therapeutic lessons of this story? This story continues the theme of encouraging one's child to develop and to separate. Only this time, the story involves not a daughter but a daughter-in-law and not a child but a grown woman who has been widowed. Naomi is herself widowed and must find it comforting to have the company of Ruth. Yet she understands Ruth's need to live her own life. She pushes her to remarry, taking the risk Ruth will go her own way, but Ruth returns the love and respect Naomi has shown her by including Naomi in her life after she remarries.

Not everything can be known in advance. And sometimes a parent must make a sacrifice to help a child (whatever the age) develop. One has to have faith that the act is right in itself and hope that it will bring the parent joy as well. A failure to do this can create a great deal of family bitterness and leave the child unfulfilled. No good can come out of blocking a child's development. This, of course, does not mean throwing the child to the wolves. Rather, it means loving the child enough to provide guidelines and support to let the child develop in ways that he must. A therapist can help a parent loosen the reins on his child to find his way if he is able, with the faith that the parent and the mature child will achieve a rapprochement.

The Bible advises training each child "according to his way." Every child is unique and needs to be trained according both to his own basic nature and to what he will need for later life, in behavior and in thinking. Emanuel Seward, the great boxing coach, has said that the key to success as a teacher is to teach the skills to the group of boxers while recognizing how different each one is from the others. Seward's principle applies in every classroom and every family.

Mike, a high school basketball coach, is a father of three. He very much wants his son Bobby to be a good athlete and play on his team. Bobby, however, is little inclined toward athletics, being much more interested in acting. Mike regards acting and especially actors with distaste, and is very disappointed in his son. Can Mike accept Bobby as he is rather than as Mike wants him to be? Mike can still try to teach Bobby the family values he wants him to learn. He will not succeed in making Bobby an athlete, but must "teach the child according to his own way."

No basic tendency in any child is innately good or evil. Every characteristic can be trained and developed to good use. No child is bad, but they do lack experience and judgment. Parents must use their own accumulating knowledge and wisdom to guide a child. They must seek to recognize and affirm a child's importance and uniqueness. The parent must teach good behavior and good character, and show a child what is important and what is not, what is right and what is wrong. Sometimes a lesson must be taught through a reprimand, a disapproving look, the denial of a treat or privilege. The child should never be demeaned or looked down on. The objective, instead, is to teach the child how someone as important as he or she is ought to and can act. The behavior may be bad but the child must be loved.

Hitting in the Biblical view is not the best sort of correction and should not be overused. Many people think that "spare the rod and spoil the child" is a Biblical phrase. In fact, this expression seems to have entered western thought with Menander, a Greek playwright, who wrote over one hundred sitcom plays, many centering around stories of child exposure. Indeed he is quoted in Bartlett (*Familiar Quotations*, 91) as follows: "The man who has never been flogged has never been taught." The closest the Hebrew Bible seems to come to this harsh axiom is a line in Proverbs 13:24, which has a very different meaning—"One who holds back his staff (rod) hates his son. But he that loves him chastens him sometimes." This means that a person who feels so tender to his child that he cannot correct him for fear of causing the child discomfort actually loves himself more than he loves the child. Although it may be very difficult for a loving parent, sometimes it is necessary to drive home a lesson which will do the child much good later on. However, this sort of discipline is very different from flogging, which is considered to be a strong corporal punishment.

A case in point: A fourteen-year-old boy with very high intelligence and superior writing skills had developed a technique of harassing other youngsters in his classes but always making sure that the other one was caught and into trouble with teachers. Two of his teachers came to realize what was happening and decided that what the boy seemed to need was a very firm, no-nonsense guiding hand tempered with a lot of positive attention and an emphasis on what he could accomplish with his excellent talents. The boy responded positively both to the firmness and to the recognition, and his behavior improved noticeably.

The verse from Proverbs ends with the words, "But he who loves him disciplines him early." There is no suggestion of brutalizing the child or, so to speak, "teaching the little brat a lesson he'll never forget." The child is still a special and unique creation of God. No punishment should degrade or embarrass him. A punishment is simply a correction on a very high-class being. Parents need to teach and guide the child as best they can. The child should understand that the way he or she lives is indeed important. Both parents and child must learn never to give up and never to *stop* teaching and learning. Parents should not say no to a child without reason. However, when a "no" is appropriate, the parent should not be bothered if the child screams or cries. A poignant example in English literature of the importance of making a child feel wanted rather than a bother is Thomas Hardy's novel *Jude the Obscure*. The scribbled suicide note left by three unwanted children says it all: "Done because we are too menny."

The importance of the role of parents is expressed in the Ten Commandments, "Honor your father and your mother." Lack of filial respect is a dangerous lesson that can be passed down easily from one generation to the next, and can damage the historical continuity of any society. Nevertheless, while children should respect parents (and teachers as well), parents should not burden the children with too many demands.

There is much that is natural in the love of a parent for a child, as we can see even among animals. Yet, one of the most important benefits a parent can impart is to enable the child to become at some point independent of the parent—independent though not detached. This is what God Himself did for the first two people He created, empowering them to act and think for themselves, even though they could and did use their independence to disobey Him. Children will make mistakes, and they need to learn to recover when things go wrong. The love expressed by God is imitated when parents teach and guide and finally empower the child to grow and be a full human being on his or her own just as he or she is. The closest bond between parent and child in the long term is found in their having a common purpose to do good, each according to his own gifts.

After all this it is still necessary to understand that a parent cannot do everything needed to raise a child. Students need a mentor—someone who can guide, support or advise them. A student was doing poorly in a history class despite a very bright mind. It turned out that he was majoring in business and achieving only mediocre grades despite his superior abilities. Nor did he particularly like business, but he felt that it offered him greater promise of success ten years down the road. What he really enjoyed was languages. He had taken two years of French and made straight A's, and was interested in starting German, but he felt that the business courses had priority. His professor pointed out to him that knowledge of foreign languages can be very useful in business and that many companies do business with Germany or France or even Quebec. The student had never thought of things that way. He could still go for the business degree if he wanted but could do it in a way much more in consonance with what he really liked. This young man needed someone to point out to him what his real abilities were and how he could come closer to them.

Love between parents and children is essential to overcome the deadly sin of possessiveness, a first cousin of lust itself, and its equally unsatisfactory antidote, withdrawal, a close relative of the way chastity has been interpreted. Hobson's choice of "my way or the highway" must be replaced by the realization that each person has an individual path to arrive at a worthy destination. Healthy parental love encourages and supports the child to grow into maturity and independence.

Chapter Five

Healthy Appetite: An Escape from the Gluttony-Abstinence See-Saw

"And you will eat and be satisfied, then you shall bless the Lord your God for the good land which He has given you."

—Deuteronomy 8:10

Gluttony is the fifth deadly sin. It may be defined as an inordinate desire to consume more than one needs or even wants. For the glutton there is no beauty in food; there is just the food itself. There is no appreciation for the preparation or for the presentation of the food. The glutton basically disrespects and abuses food, reflecting a disrespect for creation itself. This may extend to abuse of alcohol as well and is highlighted in the emphasis on how one handles his *coso* (wine) in the Hebrew saying opening this book.

The wealthy in Roman times loved to recline at a meal of dozens of courses. The writer Petronius describes in a novel, *Satyricon*, a banquet that consisted of over one hundred courses. When a Roman banqueter felt full, he would have a slave tickle his throat with a feather. This would cause the earlier courses to be vomited up, and the banqueter would have room to eat more. The Book of Esther in the Hebrew Bible describes a feast put on by the Persian Emperor Achasuerus, which went on for 180 days.

A glutton's insatiable hunger is vividly illustrated in the Greek myth of Erysichthon, described by Ovid in his *Metamorphoses*. Erysichthon wickedly chopped down a giant oak tree that was sacred to Ceres, the goddess of grain. Ceres punished him by giving him an insatiable appetite. The more Erysichthon ate, the hungrier he became. He finally sold his own daughter for food. However, with the god Neptune's help, she changed her form and escaped her slavery. When Erysichthon learned that she had this ability, he continued to sell her over and over. Even this, however, did not supply him with enough food, and he finally devoured himself, limb by limb.

In recent years it seems as though some new report on obesity appears in the leading newspapers every few days. Obesity occurs among adolescents, Asians, middle-aged men, and so on. People eat themselves into serious health problems. Rick, for example, was always a heavy man, but in his early forties, he ate himself into a body weight of well over 400 pounds. He was hardly able to walk, and he suffered from swollen ankles, high blood pressure and high sugar.

Counseling revealed that much of his unconscious thought process centered around food and its ingestion and digestion. He was surprised when he came to realize that his daily conversation was filled with food metaphors. Yet even after realizing all this, Rick remained unable to slow his eating and reduce his weight. Even people who, for health reasons, need to lose only twenty pounds find dieting very difficult.

A report in 1999 claims that since the introduction of television in several of the South Pacific Islands, a few years earlier, the number of bulimic eating disorders there had increased five-fold. Indeed a 2004 movie, *Supersize Me*, has directly addressed this theme, dealing with the role of the fast food industry in this process. Fast foods are neither tasted, savored nor really enjoyed. They are simply ingested, inhaled, and consumed.

Prudentius's antidote to gluttony was abstinence. While balance in eating is clearly healthy, excessive rejection of food may be as extreme as gluttony, and simply the other side of the same coin. While some of the ancients gloried in stuffing themselves, there were others who joined cults or religious groups that practiced extreme forms of asceticism. Some even lived a solitary existence.

Fasting has played an important role in religious history. People who are regarded as very holy have at times devoted themselves to fasting and mortification of the flesh. One thinks of Mahatma Gandhi, who employed prolonged fasts as a means of drawing world attention to his movement to free India from British rule. St. Jerome describes in a letter the case of Blaesilla, a young woman in Rome in about 400 C.E. who starved herself to death as an expression of faith and felt she was attaining a high level of holiness. Jerome praises Blaesilla's devotion to her faith and chastises her mother Paula for showing normal maternal grief at the loss of her child.

In Franz Kafka's short story "A Hunger Artist," a man billed as a "hunger artist" has made a career of going from carnival to carnival fasting near to death. Huge crowds have come out to see the hunger artist, growing more emaciated by the day, sitting within a cage filled with straw. He has always been saved by being given food and water at the last minute. When he regains his strength, he begins to fast once again, and the entire process repeats itself. However, as the story begins, Kafka informs the reader that the practice of fasting has lost popularity. People are no longer interested in the event of fasting or indeed in the hunger artist himself. The hunger artist has been forgotten; yet he goes on fasting. One day a custodian sees what seems to be an empty cage with straw and prepares to clean it out. To his shock, he finds a skeleton, barely alive and huddled in one corner of the cage. He recognizes the skeleton as the hunger artist and tells him he has always admired him and implores him to eat: "When on the earth do you plan on stopping?" The hunger artist only has the strength to whimper that he is not to be admired for fasting. He whispers that he would have liked to eat but "I must fast . . . because I could never find food I liked" (Kafka, 1996, 171). The hunger artist says he has not been fasting purposely. Rather, nothing in life has any taste for him. In other words, he has lost his appetite for food and for life itself. Clearly it is important to have a healthy attitude toward life.

Both bulimia and anorexia have become highly noticeable in modern society. Dieters may obsess over nutrition, calories, health food and exercise. Eating/not eating is the only thought that enters the mind of the person who is gluttonous or who is abstaining. Binge eating is often followed by purging, much like in ancient Rome. Anorexia has become a widespread dangerous problem among adolescent girls who feel that they can never get thin enough. Seeing themselves as overweight, they are repelled by the sight of food, often throwing it up after they do eat.

To some extent these people are impelled to lose weight by television and magazine images of sleek, skinny models. But the problem of over-eating and under-eating goes deeper. Researchers on eating disorders suggest that eating habits reflect boundary issues between individuals and the world around them. Overeaters are not able to establish strong boundaries with their environment and are overwhelmed by it. Undereaters, in contrast, have a very strong need to control what stimuli they let in from the world around them.

A vivid example of this syndrome has been presented by the noted suicidologist Edwin Shneidman in *The Suicidal Mind* (1996). Beatrice, a teenage girl, had become depressed over the impending divorce of her parents and their constant bickering over monetary issues. Beatrice reported that her father confided in her and confessed his own thoughts of suicide and his increasing dependence on alcohol. To make matters worse, Beatrice's only support within the family, her brother, moved out of state to go to college. Beatrice reported to her friends her sense of "falling into a black hole," but they thought she was being melodramatic and didn't believe her.

During this time, Beatrice began to date a teenage boy whom she thought she loved. He told her that she needed to lose five pounds, though she was 5 feet 4 inches and weighed only 120 pounds. Beatrice immediately went on a diet, which provided her with a distraction from her parents' arguing and also, in her words, offered a sense of many other things she craved: attention, control, self-confidence, and order.

Yet this sense of control proved illusory. Her boyfriend soon left her and she became overwhelmed with pain. Beatrice began to cut herself, all over her arms. She claimed that the physical pain took her attention off her mental pain.

During this next period, Beatrice described herself as "putting on a false self," and becoming increasingly disconnected from her emotions. She began to use excessive discipline to deprive herself of food and comfort. She subsequently attempted to kill herself through slitting her wrists, and was hospitalized for three and a half months in an adolescent psychiatric unit. The day she was released from the hospital, Beatrice reported going on an eating binge in her father's kitchen, eating everything she could get her hands on. The next day, Beatrice began to diet again.

Beatrice returned to high school for the last semester of her senior year and reported alternately dieting and bingeing. She "lost and gained the same fifteen pounds a hundred times." At age eighteen, Beatrice graduated and went away to college. This move helped her escape the chaos of her home life, and allowed her the opportunity to make new friends. Nevertheless, her eating disorder remained and transformed into more dangerous areas. During the first two years of college, Beatrice continued bingeing and now for the first time began to abuse laxatives. During the next two years, she went on a strict diet and had a severe weight loss.

Upon graduation, Beatrice returned home to live with her father. She was rehired for a year on a summer job she had held previously. She reported her anorexia had become much worse, and she felt her health was in danger. During this period, Beatrice came to the realization that "restricting my food intake is not about being fashionably thin. It is about my death wish that has actually never left me" (Shneidman, 1996, 79).

Beatrice's subsequent therapy sessions with Dr. Shneidman sharpened her awareness that her eating disorder represented her way of exerting control and establishing boundaries with others. "I have picked controls that are, eventually, deadly . . . For me, currently, it's dieting. But it has been other things, I think it's addictions—I've used drugs. I've fantasized about suicide obsessively, all the time . . . It was a control thing, because I was using all that mind energy, that obsessing, to avoid what was really going on" (144–145).

At the same time, Beatrice also indicated that she used food and tranquilizers out of "her need to be dependent." When asked by Dr. Shneidman why dependency was so bad, she gave the following answer:

I agree that people need to be dependent . . . but I'm talking about something severe. I would use another person the way I use dieting now, as a way to keep that fear at bay. I would use them to a point where you wouldn't be able to call it humanly nicely dependent. To the point where the other person is telling me to back off. I couldn't see the line between him and me, where we were different people. I don't think it was healthy at all. Using controls that are problems in themselves. I'm talking about not letting these things go. Ever. Being afraid of not using the tranquilizers. Being afraid of not letting go of the other person's hand (145–146).

Beatrice is confused as to her relationships with others. She confuses genuine attachment with dependency. She avoids the intimacy she craves because she is afraid she will be abandoned. She strikes first, to leave before she is left. At the same time she is dependent. She both needs and fears closeness with others. And she expresses this ambivalence, in part, with food. Thus, her eating disorder. In Shneidman's words,

> Beatrice's frustrated need for counteraction—her need to leave before the other person possibly abandons her—gave her enormous pain that she tried to treat with occasional assaults on her own body—her anorexia and suicide attempts. This is an instance where the problem is her own difficulty with basic trust. She has trained herself to be unable to trust and love . . . Can she live with a lover after he declares his love and wants a commitment? Her world is filled with people who aren't there for her—the psychological absence of key personnel. If you shut out everyone who tries, you may end up talking to yourself and feeling like an orphan (152–153).

The Bible offers its own approach to eating, which endorses neither gluttony nor abstinence. From a Biblical perspective, both not eating and eating can be bad or good. Eating should be a positive experience that brings physical benefit and pleasure to the eater and also enhances one's relationship with the Creator. It is for this reason that we are encouraged to thank God for our food, "and you shall be satisfied and you shall thank the Lord, your God." There is a large difference between someone wolfing down a hot dog, and someone who understands as he eats that his meal is part of his ongoing development and his relationship with God.

John, a salesman, was traveling down a busy turnpike in an unfamiliar and unscenic area. He stopped at a plaza to take some lunch, and felt depressed by the bleak surroundings and the dozens of people who hurried by, totally unconcerned with his existence. As he started his lunch, he suddenly remembered to thank God for his food. Immediately, his sense of purpose and meaning was restored. John felt the closeness of God, even at the bleak roadside plaza, and his strength returned.

John behaves much like the Biblical prophet Elijah, who is given food and drink when he becomes almost suicidal. With this meal, he recovers his strength and goes on to a great theophany at Horeb. "And he lay down and slept under a broom tree; and behold, an angel touched him, and said unto him: 'Arise and eat.' And he arose, and did eat and drink, and went on the strength of that meal forty days and forty nights into Horeb the mount of God" (I Kings 19:5–8).

How different this is from the treatment of the Greek hero Ajax described in Sophocles' play of that name. The suicidal Ajax is left alone obsessing over his utter humiliation before his arch-enemy Odysseus, and significantly "not tasting food or drink." (Sophocles, *Ajax* line 324). His brother Teucer attempts to intervene to save his brother, and sends a messenger to order that Ajax not be left alone. However, the messenger arrives too late to save Ajax's life (748–755).

Yet food can be abused in many ways. History offers many instances of cannibalism, vampirism, tearing up and devouring live animals and drinking blood. Certain cultures believed that such meals gave the eater special strength and power. The Bible restricts such practices. In the Noachide laws for all humankind, for example, God advised that no one may eat the limb of a living animal. This can be understood as a general prohibition of abuse in eating. Eating and drinking well can give much joy.

The Bible does not oppose pleasure in eating. Indeed, one should not forbid what God allows, including liquor: "Wine rejoices the heart of man." But do not overdo or abuse the freedom God gives man. Waste is irresponsible, cruelty is abhorrent. The Bible in three places prohibits boiling the meat of a young goat in its mother's milk. Such an act is considered callous. Good eating should be pleasurable and healthy, but the true essence of enjoying a good meal is remembering that it is a blessing from God.

A Biblical counterpart to both the Roman banquet and to extreme abstinence is the Paschal meal, or as it is commonly known, the Passover Seder. The order of the presentation of foods at this meal helps to tell a story of freedom. The appetite for food is equated with the appetite for God's mission and His special virtue. Food is employed in a way beyond simply physical satisfaction. People come together not to gorge themselves but to seek real meaning in their history. Food helps them to internalize the experience. The wine, the matzah, the bitter herbs and paschal lamb help people to relive the experience of going from affliction and slavery to freedom and to dedicate themselves to fulfilling God's purposes. This is accompanied by a recounting of the exodus story in which people question and discuss at length the deeper meaning of the story.

There is a striking difference between the story of Adam and Eve eating the forbidden fruit and the myth of Erysichthon, who ate himself. Several motifs in the two stories are amazingly similar. In the Genesis story of the Garden of Eden, there is also an attack on an important tree and a problem

Chapter 5

involving eating, but here the similarities end. Adam and Eve were not angry and hostile. They did not chop down a sacred tree, although they did yield to temptation and eat its forbidden fruit. Also, no deity tried to help or rehabilitate Erysichthon, as God did Adam and Eve. Food was the medium of punishment for Erysichthon. Adam and Eve sinned by once eating a forbidden food, but they were not punished with self-destruction through food. They can still eat well and enjoy it, although they will have to work harder for it: "By the sweat of your brow, you shall eat bread" (Gen. 3:19). Adam and Eve have been expelled from Eden but they still have good food. Production and the preparation of food will be one way for people to express their creativity and to enjoy God's bounty.

Erysichthon was very unlike Adam and Eve. He was an angry, vicious man who destroyed everything around him: (1) the sacred tree, (2) a man who tried to stop him from attacking the tree, (3) his daughter, (4) ultimately himself. Adam and Eve were not inherently wicked. Their act of eating the fruit may have been misguided but it was not depraved, hostile or cruel. Indeed, Erysichthon resembled more closely the serpent in the Garden of Eden, who sought to destroy Adam and Eve with no tangible benefit to himself beyond the false thrill of causing trouble for them. The serpent's end too was similar to Erysichthon's. He would crawl on his belly, which seems to indicate that after having induced the people to sin through eating he would himself never enjoy the full pleasures of the belly (i.e., joy in eating). For both Erysichthon and the serpent, eating is a punishment, for they can never enjoy it or be satisfied with it. "On your belly you shall go, and dust you shall eat all the days of your life" (Gen. 3:14). The Greek myth offers no resolution to Erysichthon's eating problem except his self-destruction.

The Bible's response is very different. It offers the virtue of healthy appetite for food and for life that circumvents the gluttony-abstinence seesaw. God intervenes in the manner of an expert therapist, not only to save Adam and Eve, but also to relax the strain that had developed in their relationship. The Bible develops the approach that eating, like all activities of this earth, should be sanctified and made into a form of service to God. People should "serve God with joy and awe" and "rejoice before Him with trembling" (Psalms 2:11).

Physical pleasure can enhance human holiness. Thus the Bible ordains that some foods may be eaten while others are prohibited, and people must express gratitude to God for their food (e.g., Lev. 11, Deut. 8:10). Eating is a form of expressing and contributing to the joy of life and of marking special occasions like Sabbaths and festivals. Both the nutrition and the pleasure of eating offer people a means of enjoying and sanctifying God's creation and their role in it. Gluttony is to be avoided but so is anorexia, which is seen as the opposite side of the coin.

The Bible's approach to food has great practical significance for treatment of eating disorders. Eating must not stem from aggression or loneliness, nor should withholding of eating be used as an attempt to establish boundaries. In these cases the underlying attitude toward eating is destructive, and this negative will be manifested in the eating disorders. A healthy person will have a healthy appetite, for food and for life itself. He will not vacillate between the bingeing and purging so endemic in ancient Rome and modern America.

There is also gluttony associated with alcohol or drugs. Some reduce the ability to feel life, and some offer the illusory promise of intensifying one's experiences. Proverbs 23:20–21 says "Do not be among wine bibbers or those who degrade themselves by stuffing themselves with meat. For drinkers and gluttons shall become poor, and their sleepiness shall clothe them in rags."

Genesis 9 describes Noah's drunkenness and the insult from Ham and Canaan, his son and grandson. Leaving the ark after the great flood had receded, Noah turned to farming, which he had always loved, and he planted a vineyard (Gen 5:29 and 9:20). When the grapes ripened, he made wine, and he drank himself into a deep sleep. His son Ham came into the tent and saw his father sleeping drunk and naked "in the middle of his tent," which might mean not on a bed but on the floor. "And Ham the father of Canaan saw the nakedness of his father, and he told his two brothers outside" (Gen 9:22).

It is clear then that the Bible looks askance at abuse of alcohol as well as food. At the same time, the Bible does not recommend fasting for fasting's sake. The Pentateuch speaks of only one yearly fast day—Yom Kippur (the Day of Atonement). "In the seventh month on the tenth day, you shall limit your souls" (Lev.16:29). Translations often render the verb as "afflict," meaning to cause pain. However, the original Hebrew word *taannu* implies simply "fasting." "For on this day, it will atone for you to purify you of all your sins. Before God, you shall be pure." Abstention from eating and other pleasures on a regular basis is not required or even recommended. The purpose of this one day of fasting is to help the person to overcome his over-attachment, even dependence on life's physical pleasures. He should remember that such pleasures have meaning only as helping people to pursue God's higher moral purposes. It is only in pursuing these purposes that a person achieves real freedom of will and moral force and can overcome the limitations in his own personality.

The fasting on Yom Kippur expresses mankind's recognition that their right to enjoy God's creation comes from God Himself. It is a means of restoring a high moral character to our daily lives and of restoring our freedom from gross sensuality. By doing so we are fit to receive God's forgiveness for our misdeeds and failures and we can live as worthy human beings (Hirsch on Lev. 16:24, 29–30). In contrast, subjecting oneself to many fasts or to the mortification of the flesh suggests a degree of self-degradation, indeed a rejection of the beauty of the world which God created.

Perhaps Americans have become so bored with food and derive so little enjoyment from it that they use (or abuse) food as a means of seeking cheap thrills. Witness the college students who binge drink, sometimes as many as twenty-five shot glasses of hard liquor one right after the other, although such practices sometimes end in the student's death. Indeed there have been reality TV programs in which contestants compete to see who can eat a plate of live worms most quickly, without even the use of a fork and knife.

Busy college students and people working two or three jobs have lost a pattern of regularity in their lives. Regular meals with family can be a means of serving God and of bonding with each other. Instead people eat irregularly, starving themselves for hours and then stuffing themselves on fast food and junk, often spit out by faceless machines.

On a cultural level this pattern leans toward anorexia and bulimia, in which bingeing, gorging/gluttony and abstinence are components. The tragic death of the brain-damaged Terry Schiavo riveted the nation's attention in March of 2005. Lost in the discussion of her "right to die" versus her "right to life" was the etiology of her condition. She had suffered a heart attack as a result of a potassium deficiency brought on by an improperly diagnosed bulimic condition.

What is missing in many people is a healthy inner sense of the regulation of food. But whence comes a sense of healthy regulation? It is partly biological—a person is aware of his hunger. Yet there is a psychological/spiritual side as well. If one feels secure in knowing that he has been created by God as an act of love, he will have a healthy attitude to food. God has created this bounty for people both to enjoy and to feel healthy.

It would be a disservice to reject or abuse this gift. Lack of this sense makes one feel that his health and even his existence are of no importance. As such he may starve himself, since his body is not worth preserving. He may gorge himself mindlessly since he is too dissociated to savor the taste of food or to hear his body telling him he is no longer hungry, as if stuffing his mouth will relieve his inner emptiness.

An interesting line of research on the psychology of obesity indicates that obese people are typically more under the influence of external cues than people of normal weight. Thus obese people will eat *more* than normal eaters in the presence of food, seemingly oblivious to any internal cues that they are full. At the same time, these obese people will eat *less* than normal eaters if they are not in the presence of food, equally oblivious to internal cues that they are hungry.

Consider the three following individual profiles. Patty is an accomplished and strikingly pretty woman who experienced a very unhappy first marriage, which was followed by an even worse second marriage. She began to assuage her deep disappointment by turning to food, having lost her inner connection with her Creator that had given her life meaning. She had severed her earlier strong ties to her religion.

Counseling with Patty must involve making clear to her the emotional hunger she has been experiencing and helping her find a nourishment other than food per se. Restoring a sense of direction and meaning in her life will do much to diminish her obsession with food. Hopefully, this restored sense of direction will make her less scattered and more attractive to a prospective mate.

Patty's polar opposite is Cynthia, a woman of forty-five who also went through a difficult divorce. She became anorexic, jumping from one diet to another, obsessed with calories and weight loss, morbidly depressed if she gained even half a pound. Cynthia does not like her body and has had several cosmetic surgeries. No loss of weight is enough. Clearly Cynthia neither likes herself nor can she accept herself as she is or how she looks. She can't be skinny enough.

Cynthia's problem is that she has no sense that she, like all people, has been created uniquely in a divine image and that there is no one ideal way for a woman to look. Counseling must focus on Cynthia's inner worth. Her exclusive focus on her outer appearance represents an escape from her inner being. She has no fundamental sense of being created as an act of unconditional love. Cynthia must be helped to accept herself as she is and let her inner self shine through. As she finds a purpose in her life, her obsession with her weight will hopefully dissipate.

A healthy contrast to both Patty and Cynthia is Maryanne. Maryanne neither fasts nor gorges. In her forties, with a husband and children, she knows who she is—a wife and a mother, and a social worker by profession. She greets each day with a sense of purpose. Her breakfast is nutritious and enjoyed with her family. She prepares good lunches for her children and is careful about her husband's low-sugar diet. She enjoys both the food and the conversation at the breakfast table. At lunch, she will go out for a salad with her good friend at the clinic. They laugh together and often discuss work or family and personal issues.

Maryanne enjoys coming home at the end of the day where dinner begins with a benediction and then gives everyone in the family a chance to discuss their day. The TV is not on during dinner. This is a healthy view of food. Meals are not punitive or competitive but part of personal health and fulfillment, both physical and psychological. A healthy appetite intertwined with a firm interpersonal structure provides a welcome relief from both the deadly sin of gluttony and its supposed antidote, abstinence.

Chapter Six

Prudence: An Escape from the Greed-Liberality See-Saw

"And he [Joseph] gathered up all the food of the seven years (of plenty) which were in the land of Egypt . . . And the seven years of famine began to come, in accordance with what Joseph had said . . . but in the land of Egypt there was bread."

—Genesis 41:47–54

The sixth deadly sin is greed, an undue desire for material wealth or gain. It is also called avarice or covetousness. The prohibition against covetousness is the tenth commandment given to Moses on Mount Sinai: "Thou shalt not covet thy neighbour's house; thou shalt not covet thy neighbour's wife, nor his man-servant, nor his maid-servant, nor his ox, nor his ass, nor anything that is thy neighbour's" (Exod. 20:14).

This prohibition is curious compared to the first nine of the commandments. These commandments forbid adultery, theft, bearing false witness and idolatry, and are clearly behavioral. The tenth commandment seems to go beyond the other commandments in forbidding coveting and not only possessing. Covetousness implies not a purely behavioral, but more of a psychological emotional state.

Is it reasonable to expect a person not to feel desire for something that attracts him strongly? Should a person not want a good house, an attractive spouse, a reliable servant and a useful car? Careful reading of its language suggests that the tenth commandment does not prohibit desires for these articles in general, but only if they belong to someone else. This perhaps is the essence of this prohibition. It provides a safeguard with regard to the first nine. People should want to improve their conditions and themselves, but not if it involves taking something from someone else. The greedy person may not love his possessions per se as much as the process of taking them away from someone else.

Sometimes the coveted object loses its value when it is attained. Consider the following case of Jack, an attorney in his early fifties who went for clinical treatment. Jack was married with three children and had been involved in a torrid affair with Nancy, an attractive divorcee in her middle thirties. Jack still wanted to stay married. When Jack's wife, Julia, learned of the affair, she was deeply hurt. However, she decided to stay in the marriage, hoping the affair would blow over. Nancy would have none of this, however, becoming increasingly demanding on Jack's time. She began to call Jack at home and demand to see him on weekends. Finally, Nancy showed up at a party to which she knew Jack and Julia were invited.

Julia, humiliated, threw in the towel. She filed for divorce even though this was not what she really wanted. Nancy had finally obtained what she wanted, or had she? Almost as soon as the divorce was filed, Nancy indicated to Jack that she was not ready to live with him. As the divorce proceeded, Nancy seemed to lose interest in Jack. Just before the divorce was finalized, Nancy left Jack to begin an affair with another married man. What did Nancy really want? Was Nancy motivated by desire for Jack or a sense of wanting something that another woman possessed?

The Bible recognizes this tendency. "Stolen waters are sweet," says Proverbs 9:17. However, the tenth commandment prohibits coveting another's wife even when she is desired for her own sake rather than just as a prize in a contest of wills. The Biblical story of King David and Bathsheba illustrates this problem. David was attracted to the beautiful Bathsheba, whose home adjoined the royal palace in Jerusalem. However, Bathsheba was already the wife of Uriah, an Israelite soldier fighting against the Ammonites. David should have stopped right there, and averted his eyes from Bathsheba. But he didn't; he pursued her and lay with her, and she became pregnant by him. Because he coveted Bathsheba, another man's wife, David ordered Uriah to be placed in the most dangerous area of the fighting and then ordered a quick pullback, abandoning Uriah on the field. David's plan was successful, and Uriah was killed by the Ammonites. David subsequently married Bathsheba, who was carrying his child.

God now sent Nathan the Prophet to David with a parable that would drive home the point of his transgression without arousing David's resistance (II Sam. 12:1–7). "Two men lived in a town, one rich and one poor. The wealthy man had very many sheep and cattle, and the poor man had nothing but one little lamb which he had nurtured and raised with himself and his own children. It ate of his food and drank from his cup and slept on his cot and was like his own daughter. Now a guest came to the rich man, and he had spared to take from his own sheep or cattle to prepare for the guest who had come and he took the poor man's lamb to make a meal for his guest."

David became outraged at the rich man's greed and he angrily declared the rich man worthy of death. Certainly, at least the rich man should give the poor man four lambs in place of the one. Nathan then said simply to David, "Thou art the man." This story emphasizes that although one may have a strong desire for something that belongs to someone else, it is wrong to take it or perhaps even let oneself want it.

Yet the sin of greed runs deeper than this. People can be obsessed with material goods even if they do not belong to another person. The greedy person may become quite miserly, totally focusing on the stockpiling of possessions. The classic story of King Midas illustrates this tendency well. The god Dionysus granted Midas his foolish request that all he should touch would turn into gold. Dionysus tried to dissuade King Midas but ultimately consented. At first Midas was delighted with his gift, but soon discovered that when he tried to eat, the food turned to metal. He became ravenously hungry. To make things worse, Midas's beloved daughter embraced him and she too was turned to gold. Midas's obsession with gold had destroyed everything in his life.

This syndrome emerged in Mark, a forty-three-year-old man. He inherited his father's appliance store when the latter retired. The father kept the store fairly small so he could manage it with minimal help and was able to make a comfortable living for himself and his family. He did not grow rich, but he had time to spend with his wife and his children, and he was happy. When Mark first took over the store, his father still came in occasionally even though he was retired. Mark continued to run the store as his father had.

Within several years, however, Mark's father stopped coming in and moved down to Florida to a retirement community. Freed from the restraining influence of his father's presence, Mark quickly moved to expand his business. He took a loan and opened up three more stores in the general metropolitan area. Before long, he found himself running ragged between the four stores with no leisure time for himself or his family. He couldn't keep up with the four stores and had to hire full-time managers. However, this proved to be expensive so he had to lengthen the hours the stores were open to meet his new costs. Of course, this resulted in diminished leisure time for him to pursue his own interests and to be with his family. Mark had become caught in a trap. The more he expanded, the higher his maintenance costs became. The higher his maintenance costs became, the more he had to expand to try to cover them.

Where Mark's father was able to control his business, Mark became controlled by the business. Mark was greedy and, like King Midas, lost what was most precious to him. Mark's wife became more and more distant from him and his relationship with his two children weakened as they reached their teen years. Mark felt he hardly knew them. At the time Mark came into counseling, his younger child, a boy, was finishing high school and getting ready to go to Michigan State University. Mark's wife had become very involved with a clique of friends, and often traveled with them. She had begun to talk to Mark about her desire to separate when the younger child left home. Mark was left with a business that was too encompassing and no family. He came to realize the wisdom of his father, but it was too late. His greed had done him in.

This admonition against greed is taught in the Biblical narrative of the Israelites who left their long enslavement in Egypt and went out to freedom in the wilderness of Sinai. Freedom was wonderful, but it carried with it many adjustments to new responsibilities. People began to worry about how they would eat, although they had many cattle and other food supplies with them. They even remembered somewhat over-fondly how they "sat by the meat pots as we filled up with bread" (Exod. 16:3). Certainly this was an illusion, for slaves in Egypt did not eat well.

God now promised that "I will rain down to you bread from the heavens, and the people will go out and gather each day's portion that day, so that I will try him whether he will go with My law or not" (16:4). This food, or manna as it was called, would cover the ground around the camp, and each person would gather what his household needed for that day, one *omer* per person. Even if they tried to collect more or less than they needed, they would still find, upon returning to their tents, that they had one *omer* for each member of the household (16:18). Moses had an additional instruction: "Let no one leave over from it till morning" (16:19). Some Israelites did not listen to Moses and tried to save manna overnight only to awaken the next morning and find "that it was rotten with worms and it stank." The first lesson of the manna, then, is that hoarding is counterproductive to the real purpose of working and possessing.

Prudentius offers the antidote of liberality. In a positive sense, it can be equated with magnanimity and generosity of spirit. However, unbridled liberality can be very foolish. King Lear offers a tragic example of one who gives away everything he has, leaving himself with no reserve whatsoever. Lear gives all his property and wealth to two daughters who feign unlimited love for him, disinheriting his third daughter, Cordelia, who truly loves him but will not stoop to flatter him. Once Lear is left without anything, he is rejected by the first two daughters, who treat him like a beggar. Only Cordelia remains loyal when he is penniless. Lear's foolishness leads to his downfall. But his foolishness has two aspects. First, he misjudges which of his daughters truly loves him. Second, he gives all of his possessions away.

Consider another clinical case. Richard, a man in his sixties, came to therapy, recently divorced. He had accumulated a very sizable portfolio over his many years working as an engineer for one of the auto companies. He was set financially. But he came into therapy complaining that he felt very much alone. Though he had one son and one daughter and three grandchildren, he complained that he rarely if ever saw any of them. He blamed this largely on his ex-wife, who he claimed had poisoned his children's attitude toward him.

Now that Richard was alone, he decided to do everything in his power to restore his relationship with his children and grandchildren. Not only did he give them gifts, he also signed much of his financial holdings over to them. This tendency was compounded when Richard met an attractive younger woman at a support group. He became infatuated with her and asked her to marry him before he knew her very well.

Richard's attempt to buy the love of his children and grandchildren did not work. His relationship with his children remained distant, and he saw his grandchildren rarely. Richard's relationship with his new wife had a promising beginning. She seemed attentive to him in a way that his first wife didn't. Against therapeutic advice, Richard signed the majority of his remaining assets over to her, leaving him with very little in his own name. In addition he gave her power of attorney regarding his health care.

Soon afterwards, Richard's health began to decline. He developed emphysema as a consequence of years of smoking, and in addition began to show some disturbing signs of dementia. Things went from bad to worse, and within little more than a year, Richard needed assistance in such daily activities as dressing and bathing. He needed supplies of oxygen in his house as well. It would be comforting to report that Richard's new wife remained attentive to him during this period. Sadly, she did not and began to spend more and more time away from the house, often going on vacations with friends for a week or more.

Richard was quite devastated and felt as lonely as he had earlier in his life. However, his situation was even worse now, because he was older, sick, dependent and largely bereft of his financial resources. Richard learned the hard way that one cannot buy love. Further, a liberality that leaves one defenseless and utterly dependent on others is no healthier than a greediness that is insatiable. Surely, a middle ground seems imperative here, one that preserves enough resources to maintain one's independence but does not result in material acquisition for its own sake.

The second Biblical lesson is contained in the continuation of the story of the Israelites fleeing Egypt. There is one day in the week when people are supposed to gather a double portion of manna. This is Friday, and the added manna was needed because none would be provided on Saturday— the Sabbath. On the Sabbath, people would eat from the double amount gathered on the previous day. First the people were to learn that they must not hoard and then they were to learn that sometimes planning is necessary. This is the Biblical virtue of prudence. It is also apparent in the Biblical story of Joseph.

Joseph, while in an Egyptian dungeon, has developed a reputation of being able to interpret dreams. Pharaoh reports to him two troubling dreams. "In my dream," says Pharaoh, "I stood upon the brink of the river. And behold there came up out of the river seven kine, fat-fleshed and well-favored; . . . and behold, seven other kine came up after them, poor and very ill-favored and lean-fleshed, such as I never saw in all the land of Egypt . . . And the lean and ill-favored kine did eat up the first seven fat kine" (Gen. 41:17–20). Pharaoh then tells Joseph his second dream: "Seven ears came up upon one stalk, full and good. And behold, seven ears, withered, thin and blasted with the east wind, sprung up after them. And the thin ears swallowed up the seven good ears" (41:22–24). Joseph says unto Pharaoh: "The dream of Pharaoh is one; what God is about to do He hath declared unto Pharaoh. The seven good kine are seven years; and the seven good ears are seven years . . . And the seven lean and ill-favored kine seven years, and also the seven empty ears . . . they shall be seven years of famine" (25–27).

Joseph draws a conclusion from Pharaoh's dream: "There come seven years of great plenty throughout all the land of Egypt. And there shall arise after them seven years of famine; and all the plenty shall be forgotten in the land of Egypt" (30). Joseph also proposes a specific recommendation to Pharaoh: "Let him appoint overseers over the land, and take up the fifth part of the land of Egypt in the seven years of plenty. And let them gather all the food of these good years that come and lay up corn under the hand of Pharaoh for food in the cities, and let them keep it. And the food shall be for a store to the land against the seven years of famine" (34–36). Impressed with Joseph's interpretation and recommendation, Pharaoh names Joseph as overseer over the entire land of Egypt to store food during the seven good years to help the country survive the seven lean years which will come after. Such prudence is not at all the same as greed. The purpose of earning or saving is not unending acquisition for its own sake. It is to fulfill God's will in this world.

We had come to depend on a latter-day Joseph in contemporary America. His name is Alan Greenspan and he was Chairman of the Federal Reserve. On March 1, 2005, Greenspan warned the Budget Committee of the House of Representatives that the future was being sacrificed to the present and that the current federal budget policy is unsustainable: "I feel that we may have already committed more physical resources to the baby-boom generation in its retirement years than our economy has the capacity to deliver." He stressed that Congress must cut the deficit and shore up funding for Social Security and other benefit programs.

There are people who seek happiness in the acquisition of goods or money or in entertainment or sports. All of these are legitimate activities. We all need a new coat, a new car, or an ice cream, or we may need to attend a ball game or concert and find a temporary pick-me-up in an hour or two of relaxation. Yet, simply to indulge cravings is not a means to long-term joy. Proverbs 21:17 says, "He who loves entertainment is a man of want. He who loves wine and oil shall not become rich." Excessive love of enjoyment and luxury can move us away from pursuits that are more serious and beneficial, from seeking wisdom and doing good. However, greed is yet worse than indulgence in pleasure, because a need for pleasure at some point can be satiated whereas greed is insatiable. One seeks more and more possessions and never acquires enough. The greedy person's problem is that he feels that his well-being depends entirely on himself, and he must keep acquiring new goods in order to feel secure. While all people need some amount of money and possessions, for this person there is never enough.

Wealth in itself can never make a person happy. "Blow, blow thou winter wind, /Thou art not so cruel as man's ingratitude" (Shakespeare, *As You Like It*, II: 7). A person who lacks the characteristic of gratitude is showing signs of major inner problems. Even animals express gratitude. A dog will snuggle up to its human when it receives a treat. Psalm 37:21 states that "a wicked man borrows and does not repay, but a righteous man deals generously and is a giver." A righteous person realizes that the good things that he has come from God, and he is grateful. He feels that he has been given these benefits only so that he can do good. He is glad to be gracious to others as God has been to him. He not only pays his debts but goes beyond that to lend or give to others whether the support of his heart, his strength or his wallet. He knows that it is God's bounty that gives him his wealth, and he is not unhappy to give his wealth to good purpose.

Generosity and charity to those in need is a foundation stone of the Hebrew Bible. Several verses from Proverbs illustrate these themes. The first indicates that one can gain in resources from giving rather than withholding. "One spends freely and adds more. Another holds back more than is right only to suffer want." (Prov. 11:24). Two other verses stress the importance of not oppressing the poor. "One who oppresses the poor to increase his own, believes he adds to his wealth but will only suffer want" (Prov. 22:16). Furthermore, such oppression is an insult to the Creator, who desires that humans be generous. "He who oppresses the poor insults his Maker but he who is gracious to the poor honors Him" (Prov. 14: 31).

Nevertheless, one should not give everything away, for then one will have nothing left to work with. Thus the Biblical injunction: "Let each man's gift be according to the blessing of the Lord your God which He has granted you" (Deut: 16:17). Thus the Bible seems to stress the importance of prudence in giving. Some scholars attribute to the Old Testament the idea of giving ten percent of one's income to the poor. There are two important principles in this idea. First, it is important to give charity to others. Second, one should not treat one's money or possessions so lightly as to give away what he needs for himself and his family. To leave oneself destitute is foolish and counterproductive. It leaves a person resentful and turns him into a recipient of charity himself.

Aesop's *Fables* include two tales of ants. In the first story, a beetle watched an ant collecting and storing food during the summer when everyone else was taking a holiday. When winter came, the beetle came to the ant for food, only to have the ant remind him that if he had worked in the summer, he too would now be able to eat (141). The second story is focused exclusively in winter. A hungry cicada came to an ant for food, only to be asked what he had been doing during the summer. The cicada replied that in the summer he had been very busy making music. To this the ant replied: "You chirped all summer. Now you can dance all winter" (142).

The Biblical book of Proverbs (6:6) urges people to learn diligence from the ant. Yet it would most likely find fault with both the foolishness of Aesop's beetle and cicada and the meanness of his ant as well. Of course, the ant needed to supply his own family first. However, if the ant had plenty, it seems harsh for him to have treated the beetle and the cicada so sarcastically. In another sense, these two fables, like so many Greek stories, are incomplete. The beetle and cicada need support despite their behavior. However, if the ant had other charity obligations, the two heedless and lazy insects would certainly not be first in line.

If a good person faces hard times, he can still have high hopes that his children will absorb and continue his compassion and dedication. This is more important than inheriting money. As the psalmist adds, "I have not seen the righteous forsaken, and his children seeking bread" (37: 25). The evil person, in contrast, does not give back what is borrowed from God or others, because he is always afraid that he will not have enough for himself. Never feeling secure in what he has, he cannot enjoy it. He exists only for himself. He is a taker, content to use other people to build his own nest egg. He feels he has no duties to others or to God, but that what-ever he can take from them is his. In the end, he is in a sense in debt to the whole world, but hopes to give or repay nothing. For such a person, even what he truly owns can never feel like his. He thinks all things are coming to him and is unable to recognize that God and other people are important, too.

Let us conclude this chapter with another clinical experience. Peter was a successful labor lawyer with a wife and three children. He had built up a considerable reputation and consulted on a number of important cases. Peter's career was flourishing and his income rose to a level unimaginable to him as recently as several years earlier. Peter and his family began to spend much more freely. However, as he began to travel more, he soon noticed a decline in the quality of his marital life. His wife grew more distant and Peter suspected she was having an affair. Peter's relation with his children suffered as well. He often found himself missing important activities in their lives—a daughter's concert, a son's baseball tourna-ment, and even the elementary school graduation of his third child.

Peter felt that something had to change, and he entered therapy with the intention of giving up his law practice totally and taking a low-paying job at a public defender's office that would not demand much time from him. However, this did not seem to be a satisfactory solution either. Peter had three children to send through college and felt he would rapidly exhaust his savings.

During therapy, Peter began to see things differently. First, he put him-self and his family on a budget. Then, he found a broker he could trust and began to invest his money wisely. He set up education trusts for each of his children. At the same time, he decided to cut back on his extensive travel schedule, and limited himself largely to cases within his home city. His marriage improved and he found he was available to attend his chil-dren's activities.

The true measure of success in a career is not the amount of money or the prestige one possesses but one's service to God and people, and the development of one's own creativity and integrity. There are many ways to use wealth that bring the user no real satisfaction. What a person needs to do with wealth as with any gift is to use it creatively in ways that bring benefit to oneself and to others.

The wise prudence of Joseph offers a different approach than the greed of King Midas or the foolish liberality of King Lear. Thankfully, Peter found this path, which involved not just a middle ground, but a Biblical approach that viewed concern for self and others as naturally complementary. Critical to overcoming the see-saw between greed and liberality is a harmony between what one keeps and what one gives away. Peter found prudence the proper way of handling *ciso* (one's pocket) in the Hebrew saying with which this book opened. Prudence offers a way out of the greed-liberality see-saw.

Chapter Seven

Purpose: An Escape from the Sloth-Zeal See-Saw

"Where there is no vision, the people become unruly, but happy is he who keeps Torah."

—Proverbs 29:18

The seventh deadly sin is sloth. Like the animal of the same name, one simply hangs, exists, without any transcendent meaning or purpose for living. Sloth represents not simply laziness but a dejection of spirit. The malady of a slothful person is that he/she feels that no action has any real meaning or purpose. Therefore, he/she does nothing.

Prudentius has offered the antidote of zeal or diligence. Diligence certainly can be a positive characteristic. A diligent worker is appreciated because he/she is attentive and reliable. This sounds nice on paper, but leaves unanswered the question of how one can show any real enthusiasm unless one knows what one wants to do. In the absence of such a goal, zeal or diligence is likely to appear as "work for work's sake." Rather than do nothing, the zealous or diligent person will present with a flurry of activity. Such a person will be continuously busy with one project after another. Often, however, none of these projects have any meaning for the person, and the work ethic will degenerate quickly into mindless and aimless activity, and indeed workaholism.

Phil entered therapy complaining about the laziness of his wife Angie. She was not working, but still did nothing in the house and had no interest in sexual relations. She lay around listlessly for hours. Phil became fed up and threatened to leave her unless she changed. At this point, Angie became frightened and likewise came into therapy. She promised to change and in fact seemed to do so. In a flurry of activity, she redecorated the house, redid her wardrobe with more stylish clothes, and became a compulsive cleaner. In addition, Angie plunged herself into a number of community activities.

However, Phil was no happier, as none of these activities brought him closer to his wife. The initial good feeling quickly dissipated, and Angie seemed to be simply filling her time with activities in which she had no emotional investment, but which she saw as obligatory. What was missing for both Phil and Angie was a common sense of purpose to give meaning to their endeavors. Strangely, they had never discussed having children or other important life goals. Therapy sought to help them develop a common sense of purpose, to avoid the unhealthy alternatives of sloth or mindless zeal.

Therapy helped provide Phil and Angie with a common purpose. She no longer felt aimless. She was no longer slothful nor did she fill her time with meaningless activities. They joined a church study group, and Angie took a part-time job. Now three months pregnant, Angie and Phil are both excitedly looking forward to the birth of their first child.

Labor unions and workers' strikes are thought of as part of twentieth-century history. It may be surprising then to learn that a very ancient Mesopotamian epic, *Atrahasis*, tells the story of a strike. The Igigi gods had labored three thousand six hundred years, digging out canals. Physically and emotionally spent, they finally smashed their tools, surrounded the palace of the Annunaki gods and threatened violence if they did not obtain relief. The attempt to achieve some suitable balance between work and leisure appears often through history, and many Americans have trouble effecting a healthy integration of work and play. This can lead to workaholism or to the neglect of responsibilities, to the extremes of total work or of total leisure, which represent, in reality, two sides of the same coin.

The Biblical gift to avoid both the deadly sin of sloth and its equally unsatisfactory antidote of diligence or zeal is, of course, purpose. A purposeful person has a goal. A purposeful person knows what is central to what one wants to do. He/she will focus on important goals and treat other activities as tangential and potentially distracting.

The Hebrew Bible deals with the issue of purposeful work in its very earliest chapters. God placed the first people in the Garden of Eden to "work it and to guard it" (Gen. 2:15), though not to work all day every day on backbreaking labors like the Igigi. God had already established the principle that people should work six days and cease to work on the seventh, just as He Himself had created the world in six days and rested on the seventh (2:1–3). In those first days of history, people did indeed work, although in that beautiful garden, the physical burden was not crushing and people had ample opportunity for study and for personal growth.

When, after eating the forbidden fruit, the people were sent out of the Garden of Eden, their work became harder. They could plant their crops and often harvest little more than thorns and thistles (3:18); yet their work could also be creative and joyful. For they did not have to eat only what nature offered ("the herbs of the field" 3:18) but with creative effort they could produce bread and other wonderful and enjoyable things—"By the sweat of your brow you shall eat bread" (3:19). This statement offers man an opportunity, not a curse. Work can continue to be for mankind a means of expressing their God-given creativity and of producing things that they can enjoy. It can be a means of blessing and not merely a crushing burden.

The Scriptures go on to outline many ideas and laws on these topics of work and rest—the weekly Sabbath and the Sabbatical year and the many rules on how to deal with one's employees and one's animals. The essential point is that work is not merely a way to earn a lot of money. More important, both work and rest become ways to sanctify one's life and to come close to God.

People today have an ambivalent attitude toward work. We seem obsessed with it, not out of an intrinsic love for the process of creativity but almost out of a compulsion to work for work's sake. Yet, we cannot wait to retire, to enter an equally polarized life of leisure for leisure's sake. Lost in this polarity is the Biblical connection of work and rest both rising from a deeper purpose. What we need is a desire to work for some significant purpose, which has intrinsic meaning and thus allows us to express our creativity.

We also need to rest and refresh ourselves from the rigors of work, but rest should not be merely mindless leisure in which the inner self is lost. God used the idea of a Sabbath to teach, among other things, that the human being needs to take the time to refocus his/her endeavors in light of God's purposes and to renew the recognition that it was indeed God who created the world and that a person's role in it is very important. A person's work must not detach itself from its central purposes, and this focus requires constant renewal and constant awareness. We need to learn that while God does want us to work, success comes from God, not directly as a result of our labor. When we understand and accept this, we are freed to create and grow, and we learn to leave other burdens to God.

The story of the prophet Elijah has already been told in our discussion of appetite in chapter 5. Here we emphasize its application to purpose. Elijah flees into the wilderness, weary and despondent, actually requesting to die (I Kings 19:4). God intervenes to help Elijah, first giving him the opportunity to rest and then providing him with food and drink to restore his energy and prepare him for the work that remains to be done.

Rest must be part of the entire human enterprise as a pause that is itself part of one's life's work. It is essential to help restore the purpose of a person who has grown weary. This view is totally opposed to the workaholic/playaholic cycle in modern society, which compartmentalizes a soulless work and a mindless play. Each of us needs a Sabbath—a pause to rejuvenate our strength and our sense of purpose, and to remember why and how we have been created.

A big question is, how does one find one's purpose? From where does a sense of one's purpose emerge? The Bible is quite clear on this point. Genesis begins with the idea that in the beginning God created the heaven and the earth. Then, on the first day, God divided light from darkness. On subsequent days, God divided water from dry land, created the seasons, the sun and the moon, creatures of the seas, winged fowls and beast of the earth. After all this, God created man in His own image and likeness, and gave him dominion over the fish of the sea, the fowl of the air and over the living creatures of the earth.

Several essential lessons come out of this narrative. First, God existed before nature and indeed created it. Second, God placed living creatures in this world. Third, God enlisted human beings as partners, giving them dominion over both creatures and the world. As such, people were freed from subservience to and reliance on nature.

Indeed, God has created mankind as a steward over nature. If humans can extract minerals from the ground, if they can grow vegetables in the desert sands, if they can mix chemical compounds into health-giving medicines, then they must do this. God instructed the first people to hold dominion over the earth and to enjoy its produce. They were not to ravage nature; but neither were they to be in awe of it nor to worship it. It is not nature that is all-powerful, but God. In the words of the Psalmist, "The sky declares the glory of God, and the firmament tells the works of His hands" (Psalm 19.2). Biblical people need not be bound by the powers that some people attribute to nature, as were the ancient polytheists. The purpose of man is to help fulfill God's purpose in the world.

The patriarch Abraham represents a vivid example of a purpose-driven life. Into a world that worshipped many powers and forces, including a large number of gods, the patriarch Abraham brought a new faith in one Creator, who ruled the entire world and who loved and cared for every creature in it. The suns, the storms and the rivers were not cruel and domineering powers to Abraham, but simply inanimate tools of this almighty Creator in managing His world.

An ancient story tells that when Abraham was a little boy, he saw the sun in the sky and thought that so great an entity was surely lord of the world. Then night came and the moon rose and seemed to have driven the sun from the sky. So perhaps the moon was greater than the sun and thus the moon was lord of the world. However, upon waking the next morning, Abraham saw the moon disappearing and the sun reappearing. Abraham could have interpreted this in much the same manner as many pagan peoples around him did. The sun and the moon were gods, striving with each other for mastery of the world. With such an interpretation, Abraham would have fit exactly into the polytheism of his day, and probably never been heard from again.

However, Abraham took a different path, and changed the history of the world. Abraham was commanded by God to leave his homeland and journey "to the land which I shall show you." This, of course, turned out to be Israel, then called Canaan. It was some years before Abraham found a more settled life in Beersheba.

Abraham's journey was not easy, and it was full of pitfalls. Already a man of seventy-five, (Gen. 12:4) he rejected the idol worship of the Mesopotamian culture around him and became an exile from the land of his birth. He and his family left the house of his father Terah to go to a land that God had promised him. Although he suffered many mishaps and setbacks along the way, Abraham never lost sight of his main purpose—to follow God's calling for him.

Abraham's journeys were set with purpose from the beginning. He traveled from Haran to Canaan at God's behest, working to fulfill the promises of blessing and of the possession of Canaan that God had given him. This was not wandering for its own sake or to live out some warrior code. Abraham had a mission to be a blessing to all the nations of the earth. God remained with Abraham and helped him many times toward personal growth and the fulfillment of what God had hoped for him. Abraham did not find strength or fulfillment in slaying enemies, or avoiding people, although this might also be necessary on occasion. For example, Abraham had to lead his 318 household men into battle against an invading army from Mesopotamia to rescue his nephew, Lot. One may wander to pursue some important goal, but wandering in itself is not a goal. Nor is the avoidance of relationships. Abraham's sense of purpose seemed to avoid the pitfalls of sloth and zeal.

Consider in contrast Homer's story in *The Odyssey* of the ten years of Odysseus's wandering on his way home to Ithaca after the fall of Troy. It opens by describing the frustration and sadness of Odysseus, who had to wander harassed and pressured by the god Poseidon and other monstrous beings until his men were all killed and his ships destroyed, leaving him as the only survivor. Odysseus returned to Ithaca after ten years of war and ten more years of wandering, and the myths tell that he soon embarked on new wanderings. The wandering seems to have had no goal in itself, besides adventure, and Homer and a multitude of western writers ever since have glorified aimless drifting and have rejected purpose or meaning as unworthy of the *hero,* a figure for whom it is the struggle and strife that count and not the meaning of it all. There seems to be no ultimate purpose to Odysseus's adventures and sufferings. They may serve as an antidote to depression and inactivity, but they do not provide a purpose to life itself.

This purposeless view reaches an apex in the philosopher Albert Camus's book, *The Myth of Sisyphus*. Camus argues that at the moment when Sisyphus in the Greek myth sees the boulder he has been pushing up the hill rolling back down, he experiences the highest and most intense moment of human existential awareness. This view, though expressed in modern times, mirrors ancient Greek thought in its glorification of utter frustration and purposelessness, and in its seeking fulfillment in useless, unproductive and repetitive actions. For Camus, Sisyphus's work is indeed useless, but he is human, at least, in knowing it. This is Sisyphus's only consolation, as he is not free to break the pattern. Yet suicide remains for the ancient Greek, and for Camus himself, a viable and attractive option, and the only important philosophical question.

Yet a life with purpose is not without test. The twenty-second chapter of the Book of Genesis begins after many of the struggles of Abraham's life, when Abraham seemingly has surmounted all obstacles in holding on to his sense of purpose. God appears to Abraham and tells him to offer up his son Isaac as a sacrifice. This request is completely unexpected in the Biblical account and must have been especially stunning to Abraham for several reasons.

First, Isaac is Abraham's only son with Sarah and was born only after many years of childlessness. Indeed the boy's name *Yitzhak* in Biblical Hebrew means laughter and is taken from Sarah's laughter of happiness and surprise at the news of her pregnancy so late in her life. Second, Sarah has become upset with the way that Ishmael, Abraham's son by his concubine Hagar, is acting toward Isaac, and asks Abraham to send Ishmael away. Third, Isaac is dearly loved by his parents and clearly the continuator of Abraham's teachings. Finally, God has made a covenant with Abraham and his descendants. God will bless Abraham and give him the land of Canaan as his own; and Abraham and his progeny will follow God's law (Gen. 17: 9–11).

And after all this, God asks Abraham to offer Isaac as a sacrifice? The sacrifice of Isaac would seem to mean the end of all of Abraham's work and would turn his life into a meaningless joke. His God seems to be acting exactly like the moon and sun gods which Abraham had rejected, demanding child sacrifice and fomenting hostility between father and son. Abraham has devoted himself to his God for no purpose whatever.

Nevertheless, Abraham continues to have faith in his Creator as a deeply compassionate and omniscient God, and submits to God's request even if he cannot fully understand it. He rises early on the morning after God had appeared to him and travels three days to Mount Moriah which had been designated as the place for the sacrifice. On the morning of the third day Abraham ascends the mountain with Isaac and binds him on the altar and raises a knife to slaughter him. Suddenly, Abraham hears a heavenly voice saying: "Lay not thine hand upon the lad; neither do thou anything unto him; for I know now that thou fearest God, seeing thou has not withheld thy son, thine only son from me" (Gen. 22:9–12).

These words may indeed represent the turning point in human history. In the Greek account of creation, Earth and Sky have foretold of the immutable and cyclical hostility between father and son. It is a veritable law of nature that entraps and imprisons the titans and the gods themselves, let alone human beings. However, the Biblical account cleanly and directly cuts the knot. *God trumps nature!* He puts a stop to this murderous hostility between father and son and offers a resolution of this conflict not available in the Greek account.

Had Abraham rejected God's command to sacrifice his son, he would have rejected God and fallen back into the paganism from which he was escaping. This paganism of course allowed and fostered child sacrifice! By disobeying God to try to save his son, Abraham paradoxically would have allowed child sacrifice to reenter history. However, by trusting God, and going along with His incomprehensible command, Abraham facilitates the banishment of child sacrifice from the Biblical world. Perhaps the most remarkable part of this narrative is the fact that the Creator of the entire universe cares so much about the lives of one man and his son! Abraham's sense of purpose is confirmed and this makes human happiness possible!

Happiness is not a goal or state toward which one can aim, nor can it be accumulated like money or possessions. Still, if happiness cannot be approached directly, it can come as an important by-product of living the life we should be living. But how do we know what kind of life we should be living? The Biblical answer to this is clear. Each person has a life plan laid out by his/her Creator. The truest sort of happiness is the peace and satisfaction that a person derives from working on the life plan or mission which God has set in place. This plan is not one's fate or destiny in the sense of Greek mythology. It won't automatically happen, unless a person is open to it. And many people may miss their calling and ignore what God is hoping they will do. It is not just a passive activity but requires action on the part of the individual.

Human beings must be open to what their Creator wants from them. And they must meet God halfway in actualizing this plan. Consider the example of Rafi, a young architect in his early forties who felt he was being passed over continuously at his firm. He complained to one and all about the lack of appreciation and recognition he felt. But he didn't do anything to change his circumstances, either by talking to the partners in the firm or looking for another position. One day, a colleague at the firm, who greatly admired Rafi's work, came to him privately and announced his intentions to bolt the company and start his own firm. He asked Rafi to join him as a partner in starting up this new venture. Rafi refused, hoping vainly that his situation would change at the original firm. Of course, it didn't, and some years later, Rafi continued to bemoan how unfair life had been to him, cursing his lack of opportunities to improve his lot. He became slothful and careless at work, with bursts of frenzied activity that were equally purposeless.

Rafi's passivity clearly leads to his unhappiness. How does a person know what his or her purpose is? For a person to understand what God wants requires an ongoing process of awareness—seeing, listening, interacting with good people, seeking wisdom in every form, whether in books or in the experience of daily life, and perhaps most importantly, listening to the divine call for oneself. Sometimes, we find our true life path by rejecting temptations.

Genesis tells the story of Joseph and the wife of Potiphar. Joseph, son of Jacob, had been carried off to Egypt and sold as a slave there to Potiphar, an important government official. A very capable young man of good character, Joseph was entrusted by his new master with important responsibilities in the large household. However, Joseph was also a strikingly handsome young man who paid attention to his appearance. He attracted the interest of Potiphar's wife, who tried to seduce him. Joseph was able for some time to resist her enticements. Then one day when Joseph was alone with her in the house, she grabbed his vest. Joseph was probably severely tempted, but he saw an image of his father Jacob and realized that this is not what God required of him. Gathering his moral willpower, Joseph pulled away, leaving his vest in the hand of Potiphar's wife. Angry that she was spurned, or perhaps protecting herself from looking very bad, Mrs. Potiphar accused Joseph of trying to rape her and held out the vest as evidence. Potiphar probably knew his wife better than to believe everything she said; however, he had no choice but to support her, so he put Joseph in a jail for political offenders.

What if Joseph had given in to the woman's urging? Certainly Joseph could have found sexual pleasure. Also she was apparently an aristocratic woman with important social connections and probably educated. She was in a position to offer a lover great benefits. However, such an affair would have violated something in Joseph. He was one of the twelve sons of Jacob. His mother was Rachel, a woman of empathy and sterling character as well as great beauty. He and his brothers were carriers of a great religious tradition that God had given to their ancestor Abraham, and they were soon to begin to build the twelve tribes of Israel. To have involved himself with Potiphar's wife would have violated something very important in Joseph. He would have betrayed a mission of universal importance for the temporary excitement of an illicit affair.

Continuing to be true to what he really was brought Joseph closer to long-term satisfaction. During his time in prison, Joseph's ability to read dreams was revealed. He ultimately was released and rose to a great position in Egypt, playing a pivotal role in the rescue of his family from famine. Succumbing to the advances of Potiphar's wife would have offered excitement and a pleasure at best superficial and temporary, and the price would have meant great damage to his inner being, and a rejection of the mission that God was revealing to him.

This story provides insight, too, into why the Scripture forbids adultery. Why not allow people their pleasures? Joseph could have told himself that an affair with Mrs. Potiphar would be only physical, and that he would be doing no serious wrong. Certainly, the lady was more than willing. Yet this view would have been disastrous to Joseph's inner self. Finding that sex would have no meaning, Joseph could have easily fallen into the temptation of sloth on the one hand or frenzied zeal on the other, and tried, with one intoxicating substance or another, to relieve the pain that comes from living a purposeless and dishonest life.

Tara and Bruce have been dating casually for several months. Bruce suggests that the two of them take a weekend together in the Bahamas. Tara is not certain that she knows Bruce well enough for that level of involvement at this stage. Nevertheless, she agrees to go. She comes home after the weekend feeling that she had wasted her time. Aside from issues of a lack of privacy and unwanted sexual pressures, she comes back feeling that she had been in a place that wasn't hers. The entire weekend felt extrinsic to the fabric and purpose of her life.

Money and possessions can also be intoxicating substances. If money or fame brought happiness, the rich and famous should all be very happy. Yet, all of us know such people who are not happy at all. A rabbi who has worked for years with terminally ill patients has said that he has often heard them express regret that they did not spend more time with their family or in helping others. Some would like to have read or studied more. Never, however, has he heard anyone speak sorrowfully about not making more money. We are not devaluing money. We all need it, and no one wants financial worries. However, money in itself does not make a person happy.

There are indeed "shoulds" and "should nots" in the Scriptures. These are not moralistic platitudes designed to keep people enslaved, but aids to help a person stay focused on what is truly important in one's soul and in his or her life's work. A person will be successful if he or she follows the life plan set by the Creator and will be unhappy if one does not. The more superficial false promises can, in the long run, bring great pain.

A recent example from the world of sports comes to mind. Michael Jordan, arguably the greatest basketball player ever, walked away from basketball at the height of his powers to try his hand at baseball, a sport for which he had no special aptitude. He labored in the minor leagues for over a year with no great success, before he returned to the sport in which he was blessed with such unique talent. There have been a number of explanations offered for Jordan's odd behavior. Any way you slice it, however, his behavior was terribly wasteful. To his credit, Jordan came to realize that he had deviated from the plan that had been set for him, but only after the loss of two valuable years at the very peak of his career. Given the limited time a professional athlete has, Jordan came to regret these years that could never be replaced.

The above story illustrates the developmental aspect of finding one's calling. One may not recognize it right away but may come to understand it down the road. Consider the story of Jonah, which offers another case of a man dealing with a mission. Jonah was a man of learning and ability, a prophet of God. As the story begins, God commanded Jonah to go and inform the people of the city of Nineveh that they had been acting very badly and that God was ready to punish them if they did not turn from their evil ways. Jonah, however, was unhappy with God's request. He did not obey and go to Nineveh, likely because he felt that the people of Nineveh were so wicked as to deserve God's punishment. Jonah was unwilling to announce directly that he would not go, and he tried to run away from his problem. Instead of journeying east from Israel to Nineveh,

Jonah took passage on a ship heading in the opposite direction—west to Tarshish. Jonah's motives were undoubtedly sincere—he did not feel people as wicked as the Ninevites should be spared: however, he was running away from the purpose that God had set for him, which he may not have fully understood at the time.

The unfolding story is well known. God sent a great storm that threatened to sink the ship. Jonah's basic decency, honesty, and budding awareness of his relationship with God manifest themselves here. He knew the ship was being threatened because of him and his refusal to go to Nineveh. Rather than let the ship sink, Jonah insisted that his shipmates throw him into the stormy sea. And now God reveals the depths of His compassion, understanding and patience. God did not hold grudges nor did He advocate "tough love." He did not let Jonah drown, but instead sent a huge fish, which swallowed him and saved his life, much like a womb or an incubator. Praying to God from the belly of the fish, Jonah in psychological terms grew stronger as a personality. When Jonah became strong enough to survive without the protective wall, the fish spit him out onto dry land, where he would not drown.

God again asked Jonah to go to Nineveh and warn the people to turn away from their wickedness. This time he went to Nineveh, albeit somewhat reluctantly, and persuaded the people to repent. Yet Jonah was still unhappy—he seemed to feel that the people of Nineveh were so wicked that they should not have been spared. He walked outside the city and said he wanted to die, and sat under the blazing hot sun. God again shielded him, this time with a gourd bush rather than a fish, and Jonah did not die. As Jonah became stronger, God allowed the bush to wither. When Jonah grieved for the loss of the bush, God appeared to him. God asked him to consider that if he mourned the loss of the gourd, should not God be concerned about the people of Nineveh? This becomes the parable through which God teaches Jonah about fulfilling one's purpose in life.

Jonah's unhappiness pervades this story, leading to his flirting several times with suicide. Perhaps Jonah grieved less for the loss of the plant than for not being able to follow wholeheartedly the mission that God had given him. Jonah, like the people of Nineveh, "doesn't know his right hand from his left hand." But God is not about to give up on Jonah any more than he had been ready to write off the people of Nineveh. Lovingly, patiently and creatively, He teaches Jonah this lesson, and Jonah learns that he cannot be happy by running away from God's plan for him. This story, however, also shows that there are times in our lives when we are not ready to accept the mission God has for us. We simply may not be mature enough to understand our mission at that point. But God will give us another chance to come around and to find fulfillment in this acceptance of our calling. God understands that the path to maturity is a journey. He will allow a person to grow and develop, and thus find happiness. We must not give up and leave the path of our relationship with God to grab onto quick fixes.

Ultimately the most important truth to absorb in the search for meaning is that each person is uniquely created in the image of God (Gen. 1: 27). Each person must be seen on his or her own terms and cannot be compared to any other person. When a person looks in a mirror, what he or she should see is a being who is an image of God. It may require some amount of maturation and self-persuasion to accept this, yet the Bible is very clear on this point. A human being has the unique and very high gift of creativity, and can feel a sense of purpose and compassion and a need for knowledge and spiritual fulfillment that far surpass even the smartest of animals. God will help people to recognize this.

The beloved country singer, Johnny Cash, had obvious musical talent and an instinctive ability to relate to common people, especially those who had suffered and had been written off by society. His famous song "Folsom Prison" galvanized listeners who were incarcerated in our prison system. Yet Johnny's personal life was chaotic, perhaps stemming from a very troubled relationship with his own father who seemed to blame Johnny for the death of his brother. Johnny engaged in substance abuse, his marriage failed, and he seemed driven to destroy everything he had built. At a certain point something changed. He married his singing partner, June Carter, and became in his own words, "born again." He discovered his relationship with his Creator and seemed to find his calling and the happiness that had eluded him earlier. It took time for Johnny to find himself, as it did Jonah, but God did not abandon either man.

Let us now turn to the famous Biblical account of Jacob and Esau. We do not always immediately recognize the plan God has for us nor do we always value it enough. The Bible tells us a dramatic and well-known story that illustrates this possibility. Esau, the eldest son of Isaac, comes home hungry one day from hunting. He gives away his spiritual birthright to his younger brother Jacob in return for a bowl of lentils. Esau has shown himself unfit to carry on God's covenant by his careless treatment of it and his willingness to give it away for a temporary satisfaction. Esau's behavior is slothful and wasteful and displays no sense of purpose.

Esau might still have received Isaac's material blessing, making it impossible for Jacob to successfully inherit the spiritual covenant, had it not been for the insightful and brilliantly planned intervention of Rebecca, Isaac's wife. Rebecca understood her two sons and what they needed better than Isaac did. She also understood Isaac, and she formed her plans knowing what each participant was able to do and what role she would have to play in helping them to do it. Rebecca's insight was crucial in preserving the continuation of the Abrahamic covenant with God.

Esau and Jacob were twins, and Rebecca during her pregnancy had been told by a prophet that both boys could be great and that great nations would come from them, but they would be very different. Indeed, even at birth, they were very different. Esau was born hairy (from which his name) and ruddy. Jacob came out with his hand grasping Esau's heel, as though trying to hold him back (Gen. 25:25–26). The two boys received the same schooling, and in their early years seemed to be following the same path. As they grew older, however, differences between them grew more apparent. Esau became a cunning hunter, a man of the outdoors, while Jacob was a quiet man devoted to scholarship ("dwelling in tents" 25:27). It was clear that the two sons had different purposes in life.

Each parent favored a different son. "Now Isaac loved Esau because he did eat of his venison; and Rebecca loved Jacob" (25:28). Esau was more physically oriented and not well suited for the usual classroom situation. Yet, perhaps his physical cunning and ability, if properly directed and trained, could still have helped him to a useful and productive life dedicated to God. However, pushed into a lifestyle not suited to him, Esau learned to suppress his nature and to be crafty and tricky—useful skills for stalking and hunting. And it was a hunter that he became, a man of the wilds who gloried in the chase and the kill, not one who harnessed his physical prowess to the service of God and humanity.

Isaac had risen from the altar of the akedah and devoted himself to a spiritual and somewhat withdrawn lifestyle. Esau's physical vigor appealed to him. Rebecca had grown up in a home that respected devotion neither to scholarship nor to honesty, both characteristics in which Jacob flourished, and Rebecca prized her younger son. The parents' own needs and feelings influenced their attitudes toward their children in ways that could be unhealthy. In any case, Rebecca was right in realizing that Jacob was far better suited than Esau to carry on the work of Abraham's family.

When Rebecca learned that Isaac was planning to give his special blessing to Esau, she knew that Isaac was making a serious error that could have destructive consequences. She realized that she herself must arrange matters so that Isaac would give the main blessing to the more worthy Jacob and also that Isaac must be brought to agree with her. Rebecca worked out a brilliant plan that accomplished all her aims. Isaac had sent Esau out to hunt to bring him venison before receiving the blessing. Rebecca persuaded a reluctant Jacob to bring lambs from the flock to serve his blind father and, pretending to be Esau, to receive the blessing intended for the elder brother. Rebecca reassured Jacob by taking full responsibility should the plan fail. Jacob, thus disguised as Esau, succeeded in obtaining Isaac's blessing, and when Isaac learned what had happened he quickly grasped Rebecca's point. He was tricked so easily in this mummery by the quiet, honest Jacob. Had he been fooled all these years by the persuasiveness of Esau as well?

This moment of coming to his senses was a shock to Isaac, "and he trembled exceedingly" at the disastrous mistake he had almost made (27:33). However, he realized that Rebecca was right. He gave a different blessing to Esau and full-heartedly confirmed his blessing to Jacob (28:1). It is understandable that Esau was fiercely angry with Jacob and threatened to kill him. However, Rebecca's decision had been correct. No human relations can thrive on falsehood. With the passage of time, Esau's anger calmed, and the two brothers reconciled and lived in peace, each in his own way (38:1–16).

It is interesting to consider how difficult it would have been for Esau to pretend to be Jacob. It would not have been a matter of Esau shaving his arms. Rather he would have needed to emulate some of Jacob's spiritual qualities. This points to an important principle in weighing others' abilities. The qualities that are important to one's life purpose cannot be easily duplicated and/or imitated. These qualities represent the unique spark of the divine within each person and cannot be copied.

All of us occasionally grow tired. We need time to sleep, to relax, to play. Yet there is also an existential tiredness that stems from a lack of purpose. The Scripture emphasizes in the beginning of the account of Jacob and Esau that Esau came in from hunting *tired*, and it seems that this tiredness was of a deeper sort and not merely for lacking a nap. It was a type of sloth, prompted by his basic failure to find his place or purpose in the mission of his family. He was a warrior and a hunter by nature, but he was also rebellious, and he had not found much joy in his life. Chronically tired and bored, he reacted to his weariness by selling his spiritual birthright to Jacob for a pot of soup. He disdained and despised his birthright and the pot of soup as well both in his actions and in his words. Esau would probably have found much greater satisfaction accepting that his gifts were for war and hunting and then devoting these talents to serving God. Instead, he sought to show how he despised the very different nature of his brother Jacob and further that he despised the family's mission itself.

It is important for a person to be in touch with those qualities that define him or her as a unique person. This can be done only if one separates these from the image which he or she may reflect to the outside world. Our culture stresses image, which is easily reproduced, at the expense of the underlying self, which is not. It was not difficult for Jacob to emulate Esau, but it would have been almost impossible for Esau to pretend to be Jacob. Only by each man being himself can he live with a sense of purpose and avoid the twin pitfalls of sloth and zeal.

Let us conclude this chapter with our own reading of the story of Cain and Abel. Cain, the first son of Adam and Eve, was a man of many strengths and abilities. However, as he grew up he became deeply enmeshed in the land he farmed so that it was difficult for him to give of himself or to relate lovingly, especially to his brother, Abel. Both Cain's actions and his conversations with God in Genesis 4 reveal much of his view of the world. First, he decided to bring an offering to God. This in itself was a fine gesture. However, Cain also saw the sacrifice as a heavy burden so that he did not do it wholeheartedly and did not give of his best produce. He did not have a sense of purpose in what he did.

God was displeased with Cain's approach and spoke to him—but mildly, in very careful phrases, "Why are you angry? And why is your countenance fallen? If you do well, shall you not be uplifted; and if you do not do well, sin crouches at the door, and unto you is its desire, but you may rule over it" (4:6). It was not important for Cain to offer a particular sacrifice but simply to do well, and to be behind what he did. However, Cain, as usual, had not done what he demanded of himself, and he became very distraught and hostile. God tried to make Cain understand that it was necessary for him only to do as well as he could: "If you do well, will you not be raised up?" (4:7) Cain, however, could not really understand that, and he felt that God was demanding too much of him, overburdened as he already was. He reacted with intense anger by killing Abel. Then, when God again tried to approach Cain, Cain expressed his distraught state by lashing out at God, "Am I my brother's keeper?" (4:9) Cain's words belied his thoughts—Why do You expect me to carry the burden of being my brother's keeper?

Cain's hostility toward Abel was, at least in part, the result of his mistaken feeling that he alone was saddled with the responsibility of being Abel's guardian. In hopes of breaking through Cain's destructive pattern, God finally told him that he could no longer till his land but must wander away from it. Cain responded in a phrase that expressed again the terrible burden under which he saw himself living. He is almost like the Greek Atlas, a man who feels he bears the world on his shoulders—"Greater is my sin than I can bear" (4:13). The sin was not only great. It was "greater than *he could bear.*"

Cain then went on to voice another debilitating concern. People would hate him and reject him. Cain's set of personal problems was closely connected to his inherent feelings of rejection. God's reaction to his offering may have exacerbated those feelings, and now even his land, in a sense, rejected him. "Behold, You have driven me today from the face of the land and from before you I shall be hidden, and I will be a vagabond and a wanderer in the land and whoever will find me will slay me." Cain at this point was crying out to God from the mire of rejection in which he was wallowing. So God gave him a sign. It was not a sign of Cain's evil deed but a sign that God cared for him and would protect him and did not reject him even after his great crime. But Cain must try to change.

It seems likely that he did change, inasmuch as he went on to a productive life—had a family and even built a city (4:17). His descendants were very creative and successful, inventing new technologies and musical instruments (4:20). God tried to help Cain face his problems realistically. When Cain was unwilling or unable to handle this, God changed tactics, altering Cain's lifestyle and at the same time giving him a show of support by means of his sign.

Our society often confuses laborious, unpleasant tasks with serious work. Enjoying what one does seems to be a sign that it is not serious. Work must be onerous and performed under great pressure. The Bible offers a different view, suggesting that such an attitude may be rooted in passive aggression. One should instead learn to work in a way that suits his or her own personality. If one sees giving as an unrealistic burden, he or she may not be giving the right thing in the right way. If one is truly giving of self, the sense of burden will lift, and underlying resentment will dissipate. We must learn that it can feel good to express ourselves by giving of ourselves. This is an important lesson in this highly depersonalized world. This is the Biblical gift of purpose.

Conclusion

"If I am not for myself, who will be for me? If I am only for myself, what am I?"

—Hillel, *Pirkei Avot* 1:14

The last seven chapters have each discussed a separate Biblical virtue: self-esteem, wisdom, righteousness, love, healthy appetite, prudence and purpose. Each of these virtues provides a habit for the good life that frees us from both a deadly sin and also its supposed antidote. The problem with both the sin and its antidote is that each is incomplete, either imbalanced toward self at the expense of other (e.g., pride) or toward the other at the expense of self (e.g., humility). People vacillate between one end of a see-saw and the other. Sometimes self is dominant, and sometimes the other, but an individual on this axis is trapped, oscillating endlessly, with no hope of a solution.

A case in point is Euripides's drama *The Bacchae*. Here the highly rational and repressed Pentheus tries to lock up the irrational but intuitive Dionysus in a basement, but Dionysus escapes and Pentheus is undone by his repressed emotions. Another example can be found in the Greek account of Narcissus, already treated in chapter 1. As the narrative begins, Narcissus is described as totally invested in self, filled with hubris, treating lovers as mere extensions of himself. This trend becomes accentuated in his relationship with Echo, who becomes a perfect mirror for Narcissus, reflecting back everything he says. Ultimately, a suitor whom Narcissus has treated callously prays that Narcissus himself will experience the pain of unrequited love.

Nemesis answers this prayer, employing Narcissus's total concern with self against him. Nemesis causes Narcissus to see his own reflection in a pond. He promptly becomes infatuated with it. He lies for hours gazing at the face in the pond, which, of course, cannot respond to him. Narcissus, unaware that the object of his love is his own reflection, becomes totally absorbed in the other and neglects himself. Ultimately, he realizes the object of his love is his own reflection, and thus unattainable. He pines away until death, doomed by his inability to successfully integrate love for self with love for the other.

The Biblical view of life does not assume this opposition between self and other, and indeed reflects the sage Hillel's dictum: "If I am not for myself, who will be for me? If I am for myself only, what am I?" The importance of the integration of self and other is illustrated in the Biblical story of Jonah discussed in the previous chapter. Jonah does not simply go along with God's command nor does he rebel against it. Instead he runs away and, significantly, is protected by God in his confusion. As Jonah becomes stronger, he is able to go to Nineveh.

Chapters 1 though 7 have applied this analysis respectively to seven traps emerging from the seven deadly sins and their antidotes, and have suggested instead a Biblical virtue that allows us to escape these traps. Let us apply this analysis and our see-saw metaphor still further. Each of the deadly sins—pride, envy, anger, lust, gluttony, greed and sloth—elevates the self at the expense of the other, albeit in different ways. The negative antidotes—humility, submissiveness, passivity, chastity, abstinence, wastefulness and zeal—all elevate the other at the expense of the self. These antidotes unfortunately perpetuate the problem rather than offer a constructive solution. In contrast, the seven Biblical virtues—self-esteem, wisdom, righteousness, love, healthy appetite, prudence and purpose—all offer an escape from the above traps with a solution that integrates concern for self and concern for others.

A view of life in which self and other are opposed makes it difficult to correct life problems. It is very tempting to urge a person who is polarized to go to the opposite extreme. For a person overinvolved with self, a prescription for correction may involve concentrating only on the other, and vice versa. Or, as mentioned before, a compromise solution may involve trying to achieve an arithmetic balance between self and other. This view idealizes moderation as the only solution. The Biblical view does not see the self and other as mutually contradictory. It emphasizes harmony between self and other as a goal rather than simply moderation as an arithmetic mean.

We have presented in the introduction the example of Ben's giving a gift to his girlfriend Laura. We have contrasted the unsatisfactory alternatives of Ben's sending his secretary out for thirty minutes to buy a perfunctory gift for Laura and that of his taking a week off work and spending forty hours looking for a gift. In the first case, Ben feels guilty; in the second, he feels resentful. He concludes that looking thirty minutes for a present is too little involvement (leaving him feeling guilty) and forty hours is too much (leaving him feeling like a martyr). So he decides to split the difference. He will look for twenty hours for a present for Laura—not too many (forty hours) and not too little (thirty minutes), but a halfway solution.

The Bible views this story from a different perspective. If Ben is giving a gift to Laura that is self-expressive, the time he spends creating and giving that gift will not be seen as a waste. The self and other are not seen as in conflict. Ben's writing a song for Laura as a gift will be experienced by him as self-expressive. The more time he spends expressing himself to Laura, the better he will feel about himself. Why? Because Ben's giving to Laura involves strengthening his own personality. Ben is never more himself than when is he expresses his love for Laura.

So it is with our relationship with God. Remember that the Bible begins with a supreme act of love—God's creation of the world. In the Biblical account, God has continued to deal with the world in this way ever since. When a person truly recognizes the greatness of God's creation and the depth of his love and kindness, he cannot help but be moved to love the Creator who gave him/her all these wonders as an act of pure love. Indeed, the Bible expresses this human need in the form of a commandment: "And you shall love the lord your God with all your heart and with all your soul and with all your might."

Yet much in modern thought (eastern or western) counsels, either implicitly or explicitly, against loving too much for fear of excessive attachment. Loving too much is seen as engendering possessiveness, where it is feared that the lover cannot give the loved object freedom or respect his/her individuality. Loving too much is seen as depleting ourselves, as if we are pieces of sugar that will melt through loving God or another human being.

Perhaps as a result of this, we have come to fear deep love and have come to use the term so loosely as to lose its meaning. People feel more comfortable saying that they love ice cream or their new shoes, as opposed to expressing their feelings toward significant people in their lives or to a Creator. We have implicitly accepted the idea of a compromise solution: love neither too little nor too much. Love of God or another human being is seen as in opposition to oneself. If we love God too much, we lose ourselves. If we love ourselves too much, we lose God. We search for a compromise, never realizing the solution lies right before our noses. Loving God allows us to love ourselves! One is never stronger than when one loves and is loved. The self and other are not in opposition. Being for oneself is not opposed to being for the other.

The modern idea of freedom is similarly flawed. Freedom is a term that has been grossly misused in modern history. The French Revolution proclaimed its famous slogan *liberte, egalite, fraternite*, but it led to the guillotine and later to Napoleon's dictatorship. The Russian Revolution of 1917 also talked loudly of freedom and equality, but produced only the terrible dictatorship of Joseph Stalin with his millions of victims. Many well-meaning people mistake freedom to mean the ability to do whatever they want—or indeed to do nothing at all. As a long-term approach to life, such nihilism cannot work. The Bible offers a very different view of freedom—one that can work!

Freedom does not mean simply choosing to do whatever you want. Like any human power, freedom can be used for good or for harm. Many people who believe themselves free are in fact not free at all. How many people addicted to drugs or alcohol feel they are free to stop whenever they wish? Yet it often takes a shocking revelation of how bound by their substance abuse they really are before they begin to seek help. Freedom does not mean being wholly unstructured. Nor does it mean cutting relations with family and friends. People cannot live in chaos with no order at all. Sooner or later, they will subordinate themselves to something. It can be to illusory needs, to their own weaknesses, to cults, to their work schedules or to a variety of self-destructive patterns. In the Scriptural view, however, the only person who is truly free to develop, to create and to love is the one who devotes himself to God's purposes. Freedom does not mean escaping from relationships, but in participating in them. Ben is never freer than when he is giving to Laura. Laura is never freer than when she receives Ben's gift and loves him in return.

Only by devoting oneself to God's purposes can a person become freed of the domination of both his own internal weaknesses and his own mistaken judgments of what the world offers. The capacity and the urge to exercise free will are a gift from God. The Scriptures offer high-level instruction in how to use this gift in the most beneficial ways.

Perhaps one of the attractions of sin is the illusory freedom it gives. Thus, eating of the fruit in the Garden may promise freedom. But man already had freedom as part of the divine plan of creation. He had no need to steal it as in the Greek account of Prometheus stealing fire for man from Zeus. In the Greek account, man must choose between obedience and freedom. This is because Zeus wants to keep man bound and subservient to him. The Biblical God has no such intent. He loves His creation and wants the human being to be free. In fact, it is the words of the serpent that lead man and woman to slavery.

The association of Scriptures and freedom may seem strange to many people in contemporary western society who recoil at the thought of Biblical religion, because they see it as limiting their personal freedom. The very idea of following God's commandments is wildly unfashionable in a society such as ours, which so values autonomy and freedom. Yet, is it really true that belief in God diminishes personal freedom and responsibility? Or conversely and perhaps paradoxically, does Biblical religion actually increase freedom? In truth, one is never freer than when one loves, and one never loves more than when one is free. God wants us to be free, but not isolated and estranged from Him. Our Creator gives us freedom and empowers us through His love for us. At heart, the seven deadly sins are different ways of estrangement from our Creator, and unfortunately the antidotes have often been interpreted as subservience. Biblical virtues avoid the see-saw of estrangement and subservience and allow a full relationship with the Creator.

We must ask in closing why this Biblical approach has been so ignored by the field of mental health. Therapy only becomes possible if people are free to change. If they are doomed by an impersonal fate and necessity, change is impossible. Life under the tyranny of nature is ultimately tragic. If man is ultimately tragic, then therapy becomes futile. Left to nature, a person will continue to do what he has done before. It is impossible to find freedom in a world under the tyranny of nature. In such a world, sin provides the illusion of freedom. However, if God indeed rules over nature, each day is new, and the human condition becomes hopeful rather than tragic. Man becomes genuinely free to change.

Nothing illustrates this principle more than the paradoxical story of the binding of Isaac we have discussed in the last chapter. After all Abraham's travails, God asks Abraham to offer his beloved son Isaac as a sacrifice. The sacrifice of Isaac would seem to mean the end of all of Abraham's work and would turn his life into a meaningless joke. His God seems to be acting exactly like the moon and sun gods that Abraham had rejected, demanding child sacrifice and fomenting hostility between father and son. Abraham has devoted himself to his God for no purpose whatever.

Nevertheless, Abraham continues to have faith in his Creator as a deeply compassionate and omnipresent God. Abraham submits to God's request even if he cannot fully understand it. As a result of Abraham's devotion, God explicitly forbids child sacrifice once and for all. If Abraham had rejected God's command to sacrifice his son, he would have rejected the Biblical God and fallen back into the paganism he was escaping, a paganism which, of course, allowed and fostered child sacrifice! By disobeying God to try to save his son, Abraham paradoxically would have allowed child sacrifice to reenter history. However, by trusting God and going along with His command, Abraham facilitates the banishment of child sacrifice from the Biblical world.

Yet so much of psychiatry and psychology has been rooted in the Freudian conception of the Oedipus complex, reflecting the Greek account of creation wherein Earth and Sky have foretold of the immutable and cyclical hostility between father and son. Fate and cycle become veritable laws of nature which entrap and imprison the titans and the gods themselves, and certainly human beings. No wonder that human beings must rebel against this order, often trapped in an unending cycle of sin and antidote. Yet ironically, the fields of psychology and psychiatry emerging from this account totally ignore the problem of sin. These fields sweep sin under the table, rather than attempt to understand it and provide a healthy alternative.

The Biblical account cleanly and directly cuts the Gordian knot. God trumps nature! He puts a stop to the murderous hostility between father and son and offers a resolution of this cyclical conflict not available in the Greek account. Perhaps the most remarkable part of Abraham's story is the fact that the Creator of the entire universe cares so much about the life of one man and his son! Abraham's sense of purpose is confirmed! With such a Creator, who needs to sin? The Bible provides healthy alternatives. These seven Biblical virtues are based on harmony rather than moderation *for its own sake*, and offer a better resolution of the seven deadly sins than Prudentius's antidotes. These provide the basis for habits essential to living the good life.

This is the vision that we have offered in this book.

Bibliography

Aesop (1966). *Fables of Aesop*. S. A. Handford, trans. Baltimore: Penguin.

Alighieri, Dante (1955). *The Divine Comedy: Purgatory*. Baltimore: The Penguin Press.

Apollodorus (1976). *The Library*. M. Simpson, trans. Amherst, MA: University of Massachusetts Press.

Babylonian Talmud (1975). Jerusalem.

Bartlett, John (1980). *Familiar Quotations*. Boston: Little Brown and Company.

Bettelheim, Bruno (1962). *Symbolic Wounds: Puberty Rites and the Envious Male*. New York: Collier Books.

Camus, Albert (1991). *The Myth of Sysiphus and Other Essays*. J. O'Brien, trans. New York: Vantage Books.

Dalley, Stephanie (2000). *Myths from Mesopotamia*. New York: Oxford University Press.

Dickens, Charles (1984). *David Copperfield*. New York: Dodd, Mead.

Fairlie, Henry (1995). *The Seven Deadly Sins Today*. South Bend, IN: Notre Dame University Press.

Freud, Sigmund (1950). *Totem and Taboo*, revised ed. James Strachey, trans. London: Routledge and Kegan Paul.

Graves, Robert (1985). *Greek Myths*. Middlesex, England: Putnam.

Graves, Robert, and R. Patai (1966). *Hebrew Myths: The Book of Genesis*. New York: McGraw-Hill.

Hardy, Thomas (1985). *Jude the Obscure*. Leicester: Charnwood.

Hesiod (1914). *The Theogony*. In H. G. Evelyn White, trans. *Hesiod: The Homeric Hymns and Homerica*. Cambridge, MA: Harvard University Press, 78–154.

Hirsch, S. R. (1976). *The Penateuch*. Isaac Levy, trans. Gateshead, England. Judaica Press.

The Holy Scriptures (1917). 2 vols. Philadelphia: Jewish Publication Society of America.

Homer (1951). *The Iliad.* Richmond Lattimore, trans. Chicago: University of Chicago Press.

———(1951). *The Odyssey.* R. Lattimore, trans. New York: Harper and Row.

Kafka, Franz (1996). *Metamorphosis and Other Stories.* D. Freed, trans. New York: Barnes and Noble Books

Kaplan, Kalman J. (1990). "Isaac and Oedipus: A Reexamination of the Father-Son Relationship." *Judaism,* 39, 73–81.

———(2002). "Isaac versus Oedipus: An Alternative Review." *Journal of the American Academy of Psychoanalysis* 30 (4), 700–717.

———(1988). "TILT: Teaching Individuals to Live Together." *Transactional Analysis Journal* 18, 220–230.

———(1990). "TILT for Couples: Helping Couples Grow Together." *Transactional Analysis Journal* 20, 229–244.

———(1998). *TILT: Teaching Individuals to Live Together.* Philadelphia: Brunner/Mazel.

Kaplan, Kalman J., and Daniel Algom (1997). "Freud, Oedipus and the Hebrew Bible." *Journal of Psychology and Judaism* 21 (3), 211–216.

Kaplan, Kalman J., and M. Schwartz (1993). *A Psychology of Hope: An Antidote to the Suicidal Pathology of Western Civilization.* Westport, CT: Praeger.

Kaplan, Kalman J., M. Schwartz, and M. Markus-Kaplan (1994). *The Family: Biblical and Psychological Foundations.* New York: Human Sciences Press.

Lerner, Alan J. and Frederick Loewe (1956). *My Fair Lady: A Musical Play in Two Acts.* New York: Putnam.

Melville, Herman (1977). *Moby Dick; or, The Whale.* Norwalk, CT: Easton Press.

Midrash Rabbah (1956). Jerusalem.

Minuchin, Salvatore (1974). *Families and Family Therapy.* Cambridge, MA: Harvard University Press.

Moliere, J. B. P. (1981). *Tartuffe: And Other Plays.* D. M. Frame, trans. New York: Penguin.

Oates, Whitney J., and Eugene O'Neill, eds. (1938). *The Complete Greek Drama: Volumes 1 and 2.* New York: Random House.

Ovid (1955). *The Metamorphoses.* M. Innes, trans. London: Penguin Classics.

Prudentius (1949). *The Fight for Man's Soul (Psychomachia).* In Vol.1 of *The Collected Works of Prudentius.* H. J. Thomson, trans. Cambridge, MA: Harvard University Press, 274–343.

Reik, Theodore (1961). *The Temptation.* New York: Brazilier.

Schimmel, Solomon L. (1997). *The Seven Deadly Sins: Jewish, Christian and*

Classical Reflections on Human Psychology. New York: Oxford University Press.

Schaff, P. and H. Wace, eds. (1956). *A Select Library of Nicene and Post-Nicene Fathers of the Christian Church,* Epistle 39. Grand Rapids, MI: Wm. B. Eerdmans Publishing.

Schwartz, Matthew, and Kalman J. Kaplan (2004). *Biblical Stories for Psychotherapy and Counseling: A Sourcebook.* New York: The Haworth Press.

Shakespeare, William (1980). *The Complete Works.* New York: Dorset Press.

Shaw, George Bernard (1930). *Androcles and the Lion, Overruled, Pygmalion.* New York: Dodd, Mead.

Shestov, Lev (1966). *Athens and Jerusalem.* New York: Simon and Schuster.

Shneidman, Edwin S. (1996). *The Suicidal Mind.* New York: Oxford University Press.

Simon, Bennett (1978). *Mind and Madness in Ancient Greece: The Classical Roots of Modern Psychiatry.* Ithaca, NY: Cornell University Press.

Snell, Bruno (1982/1935). *The Discovery of the Mind.* New York: Dover.

Steinsaltz, Adin (1984). *Biblical Images: Men and Women of the Book.* New York: Basic Books.

Swift, Jonathan (1975). *Gulliver's Travels.* New York: Grosset and Dunlap.

Twain, Mark (1996). *The Diaries of Adam and Eve.* New York: Oxford University Press.

Urbach, E. E. (1979). *The Sages: Their Concepts and Beliefs,* 2nd Ed. I. Abraham, trans. Jerusalem, Israel: Magnes Press, Hebrew University of Jerusalem.

Wellisch, E. (1954). *Isaac and Oedipus: Studies in Biblical Psychology of the Sacrifice of Isaac.* London: Routledge and Kegan Paul.

Yerushalmi, Y. (1991). *Freud's Moses. Judaism: Terminable and Interminable.* New Haven, CT: Yale University Press.

Index